girl on the rocks

a woman's guide to climbing with strength, grace, and courage

katie **brown**

photography by ben moon

FALCONGUIDES®

GUILFORD, CONNECTICUT
HELENA, MONTANA
AN IMPRINT OF THE GLOBE PEQUOT PRESS

To buy books in quantity for corporate use or incentives, call **(800) 962–0973** or e-mail **premiums@GlobePequot.com.**

FALCONGUIDES®

Photography by Ben Moon

Text design by Sheryl P. Kober. Layout by Melissa Evarts.

Library of Congress Cataloging-in-Publication Data

Brown, Katie.
  Girl on the rocks : a woman's guide to climbing with strength, grace, and courage / Katie Brown ; photos by Ben Moon.
    p. cm. — (Falcon guide)
  ISBN: 978-0-7627-4518-0
  1. Rock climbing. 2. Women mountaineers. 3. Sports for women. I. Title.
  GV200.2.B76 2008
  796.522'3--dc22
                          2008018576

Printed in China

10 9 8 7 6 5 4 3 2 1

Warning: Climbing is a dangerous sport. You can be seriously injured or die. Read the following before you use this book.

This is an instruction book about rock climbing, a sport that is inherently dangerous. Do not depend solely on information from this book for your personal safety. Your climbing safety depends on your own judgment based on competent instruction, experience, and a realistic assessment of your climbing ability.

The training suggestions given in this book are the author's opinions. Consult your physician before engaging in any part of the training program described by the author.

There are no warranties, either expressed or implied, that this instruction book contains accurate and reliable information. There are no warranties as to fitness for a particular purpose or that this book is merchantable. Your use of this book indicates your assumption of the risk of death or serious injury as a result of climbing's risks and is an acknowledgment of your own sole responsibility for your safety in climbing or in training for climbing.

The Globe Pequot Press and the author assume no liability for accidents happening to, or injuries sustained by, readers who engage in the activities described in this book.

contents

preface

One thing I was often asked when I first began climbing was, "How could your parents let you do such a 'dangerous' sport?" It's true, climbing is commonly perceived as dangerous, or extreme. I hope to dispel that perception through this book, however.

For my family and me, there was never a thought as to whether or not climbing was "safe." We grew up around sports, and all sports have their unique risks. My mom's first climbing experience was at the age of sixteen, climbing in the mountains of New Hampshire with hemp ropes and little climbing gear. She was a ski racer in high school and college. When my brother and I were children, we were involved in soccer, swimming, track, hiking Colorado's 14,000-foot peaks, skiing—you name it. Sports were a big part of our lives, so it was natural to try climbing.

I'm not going to lie: Climbing can be dangerous—but only if done improperly.

Most climbing accidents happen to very experienced climbers who have been doing it for so long that they grow lax with their safety. That being said, my number one recommendation for readers of this book would be to never trade reading a book for one-on-one instruction from an experienced professional. This book is a stepping stone for you to learn a little about climbing, to become comfortable with the concept and knowledgeable about its intricacies. It is not intended as an end-all instruction manual. My goal throughout these pages is to inspire and encourage you, and hopefully teach you something too.

At this point you're probably so frightened that you're thinking of putting this book back on the shelf and running in the opposite direction. Please don't. Learning to climb will be like nothing you've ever done before, so just remember that climbing is completely safe if done properly.

Katie Brown enjoying the view while lowering from the Outrage Wall, El Potrero Chico, Mexico.

introduction

I started climbing when I was thirteen in a climbing gym full of boys. My mom would take my brother and me to the gym after school on Tuesdays and Thursdays. In the beginning, too intimidated to step in, I would mostly watch as the boys—well, men really—bouldered. Eventually, however, I got used to the guys and began participating in the bouldering sessions. They would create problems and take turns trying them, and I would occasionally try them too, adding additional foot- or handholds to make up the difference in height. In turn, the guys got used to the tiny girl who was always hanging around watching and would offer me advice, support, and guidance.

My climbing experience went this way for nearly two years, and I never thought anything of it. All of the guys that I climbed with were bigger and stronger than me, so I had no reason to think that I was any good. In fact, I didn't think much at all about whether or not I was "good" at climbing.

In spite of what I thought of my ability, though, I kept getting encouraged to try a junior competition. A friend's mother was always telling me that I would do well, but I couldn't imagine that being so. I mean, compared to the guys, I was terrible! One summer, however, while on vacation in Colorado, where my family was originally from, I got suckered into trying a junior regional competition in Colorado Springs. I had never been around so many other girls who climbed, and the idea that I would have to climb higher than all of them in order to win completely blew me away. Strangely enough, that is exactly what happened, and that one competition sent me on a crazy roller coaster ride of climbing and competing, completely consuming my life for the next several years.

Along with me on this roller coaster were a handful of other young climbers, and we were to become the first generation of teenage climbers to come out of the gym and into the world of professional climbing. As I grew up, I watched climbing swell in popularity, from a tiny little competition in Colorado Springs to the ESPN X-Games.

Today there are many talented girls and boys with dreams of pursuing climbing, and there is a climbing gym in nearly every city of moderate size across the United States.

As my peers and I grew up and as more and more kids were introduced to the sport through climbing gyms, YMCAs, and other indoor facilities, we began to notice that we were, in fact, becoming role models for young climbers. And let me tell you, discovering that there are girls out there looking up to you for advice and inspiration is a strange and terrifying thing. To me, I was just me, same as I had always been, but to hundreds of girls I was an image of something they desired to emulate. For a teenager who is also trying to discover her own identity, it's a heavy weight. By the same token, though, it's a huge honor to realize that you've become a role model for those who are to come after you. I believe it was Anne of Green Gables who said, "Imitation is the sincerest form of flattery." And it's true: There's nothing more flattering than knowing that you are having an influence on girls who are in a climbing gym halfway across the country and reading about you in a magazine.

So why did I write this book? Well, for that very reason. I have a voice within the climbing community, and I would like to use that voice to share climbing and my love for it, its people, and

> To me, I was just me, same as I had always been, but to hundreds of girls I was an image of something they desired to emulate.

its lifestyle with women out there who might not otherwise really ever know what climbing is all about. While I am eternally indebted to the guys who largely, whether intentionally or not, taught me how to climb, there are certain things about climbing that are very different for women. Most girls and women still learn to climb from men, but I know I would have loved to learn a few things from a woman—such as how to deal with my fear of falling, or how developing power is different for those of us with a lower center of gravity—that I couldn't learn from a guy.

I'm hoping that through this book I can offer that unique female perspective. It is my desire to teach you, encourage you, and empower all of you—regardless of age or shape—to get involved in this wonderful sport.

Katie Brown on *Devil's Cabana Boy* (5.12+), Outrage Wall, El Potrero Chico, Mexico.

Coiling the rope after an
ascent of Sister Superior in
Castle Valley, Utah.

Ever hear the saying "The first step is the hardest"? I'm sure you have. You know the feeling: You're a little groggy, your legs feel heavy, and there are a million things that you "should" be doing, but instead you're trying to convince yourself that you really ought to go for a run. You lace up your shoes and step out the front door. One step, two steps, three steps, and you're off. With that "first step" out of the way, your mind clears and before long you're floating through your run. By the time you return to your starting point, you're not only glad that you took that first step, but you also know that all the subsequent steps were far more important than those million things you could have been doing instead.

Now, imagine this: You're perched high on a large granite dome. Far below you the rock gives way to pine trees and sweeping hillsides, which in turn lead to a river that rumbles softly in the background. You can look out from where you stand and see the other side of the valley, more trees and hills, and snowcapped mountains farther on. The sun is warm on your skin, but the breeze is cool. You are dancing, vertically, up the rock, and you can hear your partner below you offering encouragement. Your focus narrows to become one tiny pinpoint of where your feet and hands will go next.

You're a little intimidated by the challenge of the climb, and the exposure, so you breathe deeply, tell yourself you can do it, and continue to move upward on the rock. Your fingers curl over the rock and grasp tightly, and you can feel the strength all the way through your shoulders and back. Next, your foot steps carefully on a small edge and you look at it, marveling that your entire body weight is poised gracefully on that one narrow sliver of rock. As you top out, an eagle swoops past—it's either low in the sky or you are simply very high off the earth's floor. Your partner climbs after you, and she summits as well. You sit together quietly, watching the sun descend in the sky before hiking back to ground level, with its traffic and neon lights.

With climbing, that first step is not only the hardest, but also the scariest. But doesn't the sound of potential experiences like the one above make it all seem worth it? It must, or you wouldn't be here, reading this book. Through climbing you will learn so much about yourself, about life, about friendships and partnerships, about trust both in yourself and in others, about the

Lisa Hensel climbing *Mad Dog* (5.11+), Indian Creek, Utah.

beauty of the world that we call home. To do it, though, you must be willing to leave behind the comfort of terra firma and embark on a vertical journey of strength and self-discovery.

Climbing's classification as an "extreme sport" makes it seem intimidating. Au contraire, ladies! Climbing is not only safe, if learned correctly, but also incredibly liberating and empowering. Don't be fooled by stereotypes. Don't let society trick you into thinking that you are too tall, too short, too girly, too skinny, too fat, or too fearful to try this sport. You will learn in the pages of this book that there are women of all shapes, sizes, beliefs, and levels of bravery that have found a passion for climbing and a home within its community. So fear not, and take that first step! It will be well worth it.

Well that's great, you might think. *Sure, climbing is safe, and anyone can do it, but it still seems scary. Why should I choose this sport over one where "taking the first step" isn't that hard? Something that doesn't involve tackling my fear of heights? I could just take a spinning class or something.* Well, clearly spinning is not completely doing it for you, or else you would not have picked up this book—the idea of rock climbing would never have intrigued you. So ask yourself, *why did I pick up this book?* Maybe you have a child who is interested in the sport and you are concerned about his or her safety, or you yourself are curious but a little intimidated. Or maybe you just saw a colorful book on the shelf and started flipping through it. Either way, I'm glad you're here, and even though you probably don't realize it, you've already left the ground and have taken that first, scariest step.

But back to my original question, why choose climbing? The answer is, simply put, because there is nothing else like it. It has been said that there are three activities natural to man: running, walking, and climbing. But climbing is so much more than one of the most natural sports you can undertake. Climbing will evolve in your life from a mere hobby to an entire lifestyle. There is a whole subculture, or rather, family—from dentists, lawyers, and doctors to high school dropouts, musicians, and seasonal workers—who will welcome you with open arms.

Climbing will teach you about movement and about your body: how to use it to your advantage, how to appreciate its uniqueness, how to create a vertical dance. The moment you figure out that a gentle shifting of your hips will make upward movement go from

With climbing, that first step is not only the hardest, but also the scariest.

impossible to smooth and flowing will be one that you will never forget. The first time you lead a climb in spite of that twinge of fear will be so empowering that you will want to do it again and again. The bond that you will forge with friends, lovers, and family after sharing a rope on a climb will be one that will hold fast for a lifetime.

I once heard a song that had been remixed from a speech given to Harvard's graduating class of 1997. The speaker began with the words, "Wear sunscreen. The long-term benefits of sunscreen have been proved by scientists, whereas the rest of my advice has no basis more reliable than my own meandering experience." The speaker then goes on to dispense with his advice, listing things like, "Enjoy the power and beauty of youth," "Don't worry about the future," "You are not as fat as you think," "Do one thing every day that scares you," "Sing," "Don't be reckless with other people's hearts or let others be reckless with yours," etc. At one point he says, "Enjoy your body. Use it every way you can. Don't be afraid of it or what other people think of it. It's the greatest instrument you'll ever own."

In this age of constantly striving for outward perfection, are you a woman who wants to live out these words? Are you a woman who wants to become intimately acquainted with how fabulous and intricate the human body is? Do you have an innate desire to push yourself and your comfort level to "do one thing every day that scares you"? Are you a woman who wishes to

Climbing is not only safe . . . but also incredibly liberating and empowering.

pass that confidence and strength down to her daughter or son? A woman who longs to revel in the fact that yesterday she was summiting a sandstone tower but today is in the office in heels, or teaching math to high school students, or building sand castles with her three-year-old?

If you are any of these things, then climbing is for you. In its essence, climbing will change your life—and that is where this book comes into play. It will teach you not only practical lessons such as how to tie a knot, or how to "drop knee," but also how to deal with your fear and how climbing's psychology can apply to your everyday life. This book's goal is not only to instruct, but also to inspire, challenge, and encourage you along your quest.

So as you turn this page, remember: It is not at the destination that the lesson is learned, it is during the journey. Journey on then—one step at a time!

interview

Sean Patrick is the founder of HERA Women's Cancer Foundation (www.herafoundation.org). Sean is a woman whose strength and courage in the face of insurmountable odds have inspired all of us within the climbing community. Several years ago she was life-flighted out of Yosemite Valley and given four to six weeks to live. Her disease: ovarian cancer. In spite of her prognosis, she forged ahead, sought out doctors on the cutting edge of science, and participated in

several experimental treatments. Today she is not only still with us, but has started the Climb4Life, an event designed to bring women together to climb and raise awareness of ovarian cancer.

Tell me how you got started climbing and how old you were.
I was thirty-nine and had just gone through a divorce. It was my gift to myself. I took a class from Colorado Mountain College—Intro to Rock Climbing. I was hooked.

How has climbing, its community, and its culture affected your life?
I had always been athletic, so sports have been an important part of my life. Once I started climbing, though, it became so much more than just a physical activity. It became a way of looking at the world—a lifestyle. Climbing taught and continues to teach me so much about myself and my tolerance for risk and challenge. It is a touchstone that puts the world around me into perspective. The skills that I have learned in climbing—solving the problem, looking at an obstacle from many angles, pushing past where you think you can go mentally and physically, and making tough decisions—are all the building blocks for success in anything one does.

Sean Patrick climbing at the HERA Climb4Life in Red Rocks, Nevada.

In addition, the generosity and spirit of the climbing community is inspiring. No matter where I have traveled to climb, I have met amazing people who have openly welcomed me into their community. It never mattered what level I was climbing at, which has varied widely, given all I have been through in the past few years.

My fear serves as a teacher that lets me examine what is going on in a bigger context in my life.

Are you ever scared? How do you deal with that fear?

I unfortunately have always had severe performance anxiety. It has held me back on occasion—I'll know I can do something but my mind just shuts me down. So, yes, I am scared. To deal with that fear, I try to break the climb into manageable sections—this keeps me from getting ahead of myself and freaking out before I've even gotten to the most difficult section (aka the "crux").

I also give myself permission to back off, which may mean that on that particular day, I'm going to come down and plan to come back on another day when I'm feeling more mentally prepared. Sometimes, though, there are situations where you can't back off, in which case I do a lot of deep breathing and centering. I try to find a resting place for my body and mind that allows me to collect myself and go forward.

Funny—how I climb on any given day is a window into my tolerance for risk at that particular moment. My fear serves as a teacher that lets me examine what is going on in a bigger context in my life.

How did climbing play a part in your fight with cancer?

Being diagnosed with cancer is like finding yourself on a climb that has gone really bad—the worst "epic," if you will. There are no answers, and you find you must navigate the disease by dealing with what is in your face and not how you wish it would be. The physical and mental stress can be overwhelming. The skills I learned in climbing—going when you don't want to go, preparation, understanding as much as you can about what you may be up against, perseverance, finding you can go a whole lot further than you think you can go—these have all been invaluable during my journey with cancer.

I was unfortunately diagnosed with a rare form of the disease, so I have undergone many major abdominal surgeries and several clinical trials—but I have continued to climb throughout the process. It has kept me sane and continues to be my touchstone. Climbing teaches me to believe in myself. Life is so finite and precious—it is the moments you experience and the people you share them with that are real. The rest is just fluff, filler. And when you get in that primal place where the world is simply measured in life and death, climbing is someplace where you can find out what really matters and what does not.

What has climbing taught you?
The greatest lesson has been to follow my passion—when I am in that zone, doing what I love, everything is right with the world. That does not mean it comes without struggle and hard work, but it makes for a rewarding journey. The cause of death is birth, and we are given the time in between to live—some of us get longer than others. I say make it count by doing what you love.

What would you like to pass on to women out there who are intrigued by climbing but intimidated as well?
Just do it. Go to your local climbing gym and take a class. It is a safe and controlled environment where you can get a feel for it and decide whether or not it's something you want to pursue. Or, if you are feeling more adventurous, there are lots of destination women's clinics where you can combine a vacation with learning a new skill.

Katie Brown not crying on
Weeping Jesus (5.12d), El
Potrero Chico, Mexico.

So, you're convinced, and you're ready to "take the plunge." But where to begin? Well, before I begin, let me start by saying three things:

1. Rock climbing does not require big muscles.
2. By being a woman, you are already at an advantage.
3. Being tied to a rope and stuck to the side of a cliff will be one of the most liberating and empowering experiences of your life.

These statements seem contradictory to your perception of what rock climbing is, right? Keep reading and I will explain to you why the above assertions are true. I'm going to keep referring to these statements throughout the book, so don't forget them.

Head to the Climbing Gym

First, I would suggest taking Sean's advice from the interview in the previous chapter, and head to your local gym. Most major towns and cities across the United States have at least one climbing gym; a list can be found in appendix B. There are also more and more climbing walls popping up in traditional gyms, so be sure to check at your local 24 Hour Fitness or Gold's Gym as well.

Attend a Climbing School or Clinic

If the gym option doesn't pan out, there are many private instructors, clinics, and guiding schools to be found. The programs operating outside your town will not only teach you how to climb, but will give you the opportunity to travel to a new and exciting destination and meet climbers from all over the country. Attending a women's-only clinic will give you the opportunity to meet other women interested in the sport and will teach you things specific to women, such as how to use technique instead of brute muscle. See appendix C for a list of climbing schools and appendix D for women-specific events.

Exercise

If, however, you're nervous about just rushing to the gym or a class, there are a few exercises that you can do to help prepare your body for the demands of climbing.

Strengthen Your Fingers

It really helps in climbing to have strong fingers. This sounds like a tiny part of the body,

Katie Brown on *Air Swedin*, a hard 5.13R at Indian Creek, Utah.

Lisa Hensel packing up after a day of bouldering at the Buttermilk Boulders near Bishop, California.

but it's true. Quite often you'll be holding on to tiny edges, so the stronger your fingers are, the better off you'll be. Try picking up a stress ball at your local office-supply store and squeezing it while sitting at your desk. You'll get a bit of finger strength and maybe relieve some stress while you're at it.

Work on Your Back, Arms, and Shoulders

Climbing won't cause you to bulk up, so don't worry. I'm not going to tell you to go lift heavy weights at the gym. When climbing, you are continually pulling your body weight around, which isn't going to give you big muscles. Your legs don't get bulky muscles from walking your body around everywhere, do they? That being said, the most you'll need to prepare for climbing is a pull-up bar. If you can do a pull-up, great, but a lot of women can't. Try just hanging, straight-arm, for as long as you can. Or, do some light lifting to start strengthening your shoulders, biceps, lats, and back.

Go for a Run

Climbing is going to make you huff and puff (if it doesn't, you're probably holding your breath and will need to focus on breathing—but we'll get to that later), so being cardio-vascularly fit is going to help immensely.

Find a Climbing Partner

Climbing is generally considered an individual sport. When you're up on the rock, that's it—just you and the rock, negotiating with each other. Problem is, you can't climb without a partner, and often just having someone on the ground encouraging you and offering advice will help you remember all the different things that you are going to be trying to think about all at once.

Climbing is a challenging sport, no doubt about it. Some sports require endurance, some call for pure guts, and some demand skill and precision, but climbing has it all. So after that first lesson at the climbing gym, it's ideal to have a regular partner to keep you going back, not to mention being there to tell you that your body looks a bit off-balance on the move you've been struggling with and to suggest putting your left foot a little higher.

The problem with this scenario is that too often the easiest solution is to climb with your significant other. While this may sound convenient and even romantic, it's often not a good idea. This is particularly true if that significant other is already a climber. Being a skilled climber and being a skilled teacher are not synonymous. Here are some classic phrases heard by climbing couples:

"Just shut up and belay."

"I SAID 'take'!"

"Why aren't you listening to me?"

"Pay attention! You're not watching me!"

"Just try using that hold . . . why don't you just try it my way?"

"Less talking, more climbing."

"What do I have to do to make you stop telling me what to do?"

Hiking out after a day of sport climbing at Smith Rock, Oregon.

Needless to say, being lovers and climbing partners can be ruthless. That's not to say that such a scenario won't work for you, but generally speaking, you're better off climbing with—and especially *learning* to climb with—someone other than that special someone.

Recruit a Friend

Do you have a friend who is also intrigued by climbing? Try recruiting her or him in your newfound pursuit of learning to climb. A good friend will make the ideal climbing partner, and it's always fun to learn a new skill with someone who is equally as baffled as you are.

Join a Club or Team

Many climbing gyms have climbing clubs or teams, even ones that are specifically for women. Try finding out if such a group exists at your gym, and if it doesn't, maybe it's time to start one. I, for one, started meeting several girlfriends at my gym twice a week, and it was an evening of laughing and climbing that I always looked forward to.

Take a Class

Taking a climbing class will not just give you an advantage over trying to learn to climb on your own—it's also a great way to meet people who share your passions. You can even participate in courses that will take you to unique places all over the United States and beyond (see appendix D).

FAQs

What equipment will I need?

For your first few trips to the gym, you will be able to rent the necessary shoes and harness. Once you've decided that you cannot live without this sport, however, it's best to invest in your own setup. There are many brands of harnesses that are specifically designed for a woman's body. As for shoes, they are going to be the most important part of your climbing equipment, so it's important to do your research and make sure you get a pair that fit you just right. Climbing shoes are generally worn sockless, and you want them to fit like ballet slippers. The better they form to your feet, the easier it's going to be for you to feel the tiny nubbins that you may be stepping on.

Another item you may choose to include in your initial setup is a chalk bag. Climbers use chalk in a fashion similar to gymnasts. The chalk helps to dry the sweat off your hands, thereby giving you a better grip on your handholds. A chalk bag is worn on a belt around your waist and hangs from your backside so that it's easy to reach for a dip with either hand.

Finally, you may want to invest in your own belay device. (Belaying is the act of holding your partner's rope and catching her if she falls.) There are many different kinds of belay devices, but they all work in basically the same manner. You will also need a locking carabiner to affix the belay device to your harness. With this setup, you will be ready to go.

When sport climbing, you clip the rope to a quickdraw attached to a bolt drilled permanently into the rock. Several feet up clip again in the same way, continuing to do so until you reach a bolted anchor at the top of the climb.

How does the rope get up there?

Climbing indoors is one thing, but when climbing outdoors, this is a common question of passersby. To get the rope "up there," the first climber must climb while trailing the rope below her. This person is known as the lead climber. On a bolted, or sport, route there are bolts that have been drilled into the rock at regular intervals. Affixed to the bolt is a loop of very strong metal with a hole in it. The lead climber carries a quickdraw, which is a length of webbing that attaches the carabiners to each other. The leader will clip one carabiner to the bolt, and then clip her rope into the other end. This means that were the lead climber to fall, she would fall below her last quickdraw equal to the distance that she was above it. Once the leader gets to the top of a route, there will be two bolts drilled next to each other, often with lengths of chain attached to them. This is the anchor, and the leader will clip one quickdraw to each bolt, clip the rope into both, and then be lowered back to the ground by her belayer. The climb is now ready to toprope.

If I can't even do a pull-up, how am I going to haul my whole body up a wall?

Climbing involves so much more than just pure strength. I started climbing when I was thirteen and couldn't do any pull-ups for at least the first two years. A lack of pure strength can sometimes actually be an asset, because you are forced to rely on your technique, your legs, and your feet to help you get up, and ultimately this will be far more beneficial than just being strong.

How does belaying work, and is it safe?

When a climber is tied to one end of a rope, the person holding the other end to catch the climber is known as a belayer. There are different techniques for lead belaying and toprope belaying, so it is important to learn each before using either. Belaying is very safe if done properly. The belayer uses a device to catch the climber. There are many different ones, but the most common are an ATC or a Grigri. Again, both work a bit differently, and it's important to learn how to use each one independently. The fundamental idea of how they work, however, is

An example of a belayer giving an attentive, safe belay. Her hand is on the brake as she watches the climber and gives slack with which to clip.

the same. A locking carabiner attaches the belay device, harness, and rope together, and when the climber falls, the belayer activates the locking mechanism of the belay device, which locks down on the rope and catches the climber.

This is the perfect "fall like a cat" body position. Stay relaxed but still prepared for the direction in which your body will fall.

What happens if I fall off?

If you are on toprope when you fall off, that's all that will happen: You'll fall off. The rope will catch you, and you'll find yourself dangling in the air. Depending on rope stretch, you may sink up to six inches, but rarely more. The rope will hold you in position so that when you're ready to try again, you can start at the same point you fell from, regardless of how high off the ground you are.

What's the difference between rock climbing and mountain climbing?

Rock climbing and mountain climbing are often confused with one another, and for good reason: They use much of the same language and tools. There is a pretty big difference between the two, however. I often get asked, "Are you ever going to climb Everest?" when people find out that I'm a climber. The answer, my friends, is a resounding NO! I hate being cold.

Rock climbing is basically just what it sounds like. We climb cliffs and walls that are formed by rivers, mountains, or other natural forces, but the style of climbing that we do is very gymnastic. Often we only climb fifty feet up the side of a cliff, or up a ten-foot boulder. Essentially, we climb rocks purely for the sake of the challenge and the movement.

Will rock climbing give me bulky muscles?

The simple answer is no. The complicated answer has something to do with the fact that you are lifting your body weight. To build bulk, you have to do short, repetitive movements within an isolated muscle group. Climbing, on the other hand, uses multiple muscle groups to achieve one graceful, coordinated movement. Climbing is like a vertical dance. Are dancers bulky? Or how about yoga? Similar muscle groups are used, but does yoga build bulk? All three activities involve the act of lifting and moving your own body weight. Climbing involves reaching, stretching, and strengthening all in one, so it can actually lengthen your muscles, creating a slender, toned look.

Is rock climbing expensive?

Climbing does involve an initial expense for equipment and a climbing-gym membership. Compared to other sports, however, it is relatively inexpensive. Your equipment will last you anywhere from one to five or more years, and better yet, once you're comfortable with your skills in the gym, you can move to climbing outdoors (which we will talk about later), where no membership fee is required!

What if I'm afraid of heights?

A lot of climbers are afraid of heights. In fact, a lot of people in general are afraid of heights. This doesn't necessarily mean that climbing isn't for you or that you will hate it—it just means that you may have an added challenge to overcome. But, oh, what a feeling it will be when you do! For starters, begin slowly. Even if you only make it five or ten feet off the ground, that's okay. Start there, and each day try to go a few inches higher. Try hanging from the rope and learning to trust both it and your belayer. Consciously concentrate on your body and its vertical dance rather than on how high

Climbing involves reaching, stretching, and strengthening all in one, so it can actually lengthen your muscles, creating a slender, toned look.

you are. Focus your mind on the next hold, and treat it like any big, overwhelming task. Just one move—that's all you have to do. Keep your focus on what's ahead of you rather than looking down to see what is below you.

I don't have the body type of a gymnast or ballet dancer. Will I still be able to climb?

Women of all sizes, shapes, ages, and levels of fitness can climb. You may never be a world-class climber, but that's not what you're looking for anyway, is it? Just because you're not going to be the "best" at it doesn't mean you can't enjoy the challenge and workout. Furthermore, climbing relies heavily on technique—that is what is so great about the sport. There are no hard and fast "rules" for how it's done. Everyone's body is different, and everyone can learn to adapt her shape to the climb that is in front of her. Over time you will learn what techniques work or don't work for your body and its possible limitations. You will also learn what techniques you can employ to help compensate for any potential limitations that you may have.

What are the big mattresses that I see some climbers carrying around on their backs?

The mattresses are called "crash pads" and are for bouldering, which is a kind of climbing that does not require a rope. Bouldering is exactly what it sounds like—climbing on boulders. Boulder problems vary in height, anywhere from two to twenty feet, and crash pads are laid on the ground so that when a climber falls or jumps, he or she lands safely. Bouldering also requires a partner for spotting, which is the act of standing below a climber and helping to guide her to the ground. How to properly spot your partner will be covered later in the book.

Can my children try climbing? Is it safe for them?

Children love and often excel at climbing. I began climbing at the age of thirteen and feel very lucky that I got to start at such a young age. Like many sports, it is easier to learn a new skill when you are still a child.

It is always a good idea to have an adult supervisor around when your kids are climbing, but it is absolutely safe for them to try, and they can even learn how to spot and belay each other. There are many clubs, teams, and organizations available for kids today, including a competitive climbing circuit for youths.

interview

Amanda Woods is a sixteen-year-old in Colorado who has been climbing for eleven years. She climbs with her mother, father, and brother on a regular basis.

How has climbing impacted your life?

It's more like climbing is my life. While I work hard in school and participate in church and various other activities, my focus is completely on climbing. Instead of spending my days watching TV and playing on the computer, I'm out in the mountains climbing rocks. Climbing has become my lifestyle more than anything else. To be quite honest, I can't imagine my life away from the rocks—regardless of whether they're real or plastic.

How has climbing affected your relationship with your mom?

With my mom, it's just another way to bond. Even though she's sometimes intimidated by climbing, she still does it, and I respect her for facing her fears. In the gym I like to give her beta and help her improve her skills. Climbing with either of my parents just feels like we are building on our relationship and trust every day, and it's a great feeling to be getting closer to them.

Amanda Woods bouldering in Rocky Mountain National Park, Colorado.

What do you like about climbing?

I love the fact that it feels so natural. There's nothing superficial about it. It's just me and the rock, with nothing but air in between. The difference between just a regular life and climbing is the fact that it can't even be considered a sport so much as it's a way of life that not that many people live. As my mom and dad both say to me, it's not a competition with an opponent, it's a battle against you and the rock—even at competitions. There's nothing else like it.

Do you ever get scared? How do you deal with that?

Of course I do. The fear of heights is one of my greatest phobias, but the only way I can get over that is by pushing my limits. Mentally I don't tend to be strong at all, but if I tell myself that physically I can do something and that nothing is going to happen, I can feel some sort of relief—but most of the time it just takes a few tries and a lot of pep talks from my parents.

What is your favorite climbing memory with your mom?

I remember climbing in Rifle, Colorado, with my mom. I had set up *Hot Potato* (5.7) for her. It was my first lead climb there, and she followed right after with the send. She has a worse fear of heights than I do, so seeing her accomplishment was very inspirational at the time.

What keeps you climbing as a family?

Why, the fun of course. The fact that we can go out whenever we want and climb some cool stuff. It's also nice knowing that you always have a climbing partner to go out with. It's an activity that takes commitment and a lot of hard work, so it's perfect for us all to go out and push each other and just hang out.

How do you help motivate or inspire each other?

Inspiration comes from everyone cheering you on when you're about to send. It comes from my mom and dad showing up at every one of my competitions to add their support. But most of all, it comes from the things I have experienced with these people and the things I can't wait to do in the future.

What's the best thing about having your mother as a climbing partner?

I know I can trust my mom and always have her there with me for support. We may fight occasionally, but we'll always just head back into the mountains and everything will just seem to work itself out.

Do you think you'll still be climbing in ten years?

I'll be climbing to the grave.

Katie Brown upside down on *Nosferatu* (5.12c) in a crazy-steep cave near El Salto, Mexico.

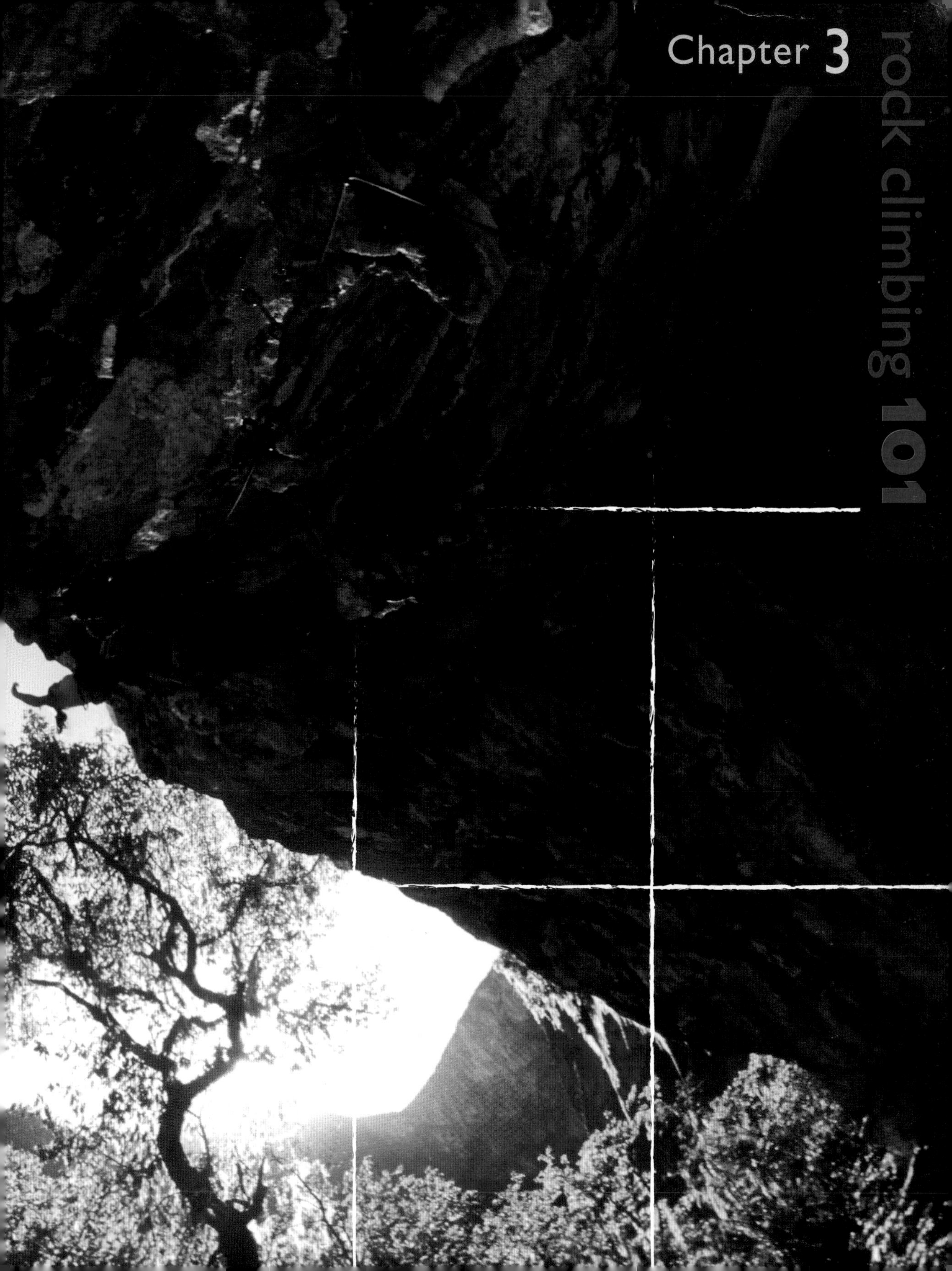

Chapter 3

For most sports, there exists a set of rules that apply to everyone across the board, and the trick is to improve at those set of rules or your skills. But climbing is another story. The same route climbed by several different people could look very different, depending on style, body type, and innumerable other variables. Think of it as math versus English. In math, once you learn a rule, it stays the same, no matter what. In English, however, a certain rule can be changed or bent, based on things such as "artistic license."

There are, however, a few skills and techniques that are guaranteed to work, as well as some important things to know. First, it's important to know how to tie your knot and thread and use your belay device. Any climbing gym across the country will be able to teach you these skills. Second, it's important to learn the commands that were created so that you and your climbing partner can check and re-check all of your safety points. And third, you will need to know the basic body positions required to use your entire body to the best of your ability.

Commands

Before climbing, you and your partner will exchange a series of statements designed to clarify that both parties are ready to start climbing and that all systems have been checked. These commands are as follows:

> CLIMBER: On belay?
> BELAYER : Belay on.
> CLIMBER: Climbing.
> BELAYER: Climb on.

Other commands:

- **Take:** I'm tired and want to hang on the rope for a bit to recover.

- **Falling:** Obvious, right?

- **Slack:** A way of telling your belayer that you need more slack in the rope. It's common to think that the tighter the rope, the better, but often this is not the case. If you are toproping a steep climb, for example, a too tight rope can actually pull you off. The same goes for lead climbing.

- **Up rope:** There is too much slack in the rope and I need a little more tension.

- **Clipping:** Alerting your belayer that you are about to clip your rope into a quickdraw and will need a couple armloads of slack. (This command is only used for lead climbing.)

- **Watch me:** This part of the climb is extra hard and/or scary, so you are asking the belayer to pay extra close attention to you.

Opposite (left to right): Pull with your left hand while pushing with your right foot to keep yourself balanced and tucked into the rock. If you try to pull and push with the same hand (center and right photos), you will swing and fall off.

Body Positions

When you think of climbing, you may visualize the movement of climbing a ladder. Once you have the opportunity to actually observe other climbers, though, you will notice that climbing is not nearly that static. Climbing involves a great deal of twisting, turning, and other dance-like movements. In fact, climbing has actually been equated to a vertical dance.

The idea of a vertical dance once again dispels a common myth surrounding climbing: that it is a thugging, aggressive, "extreme" sport performed by men with big, bulky muscles. The fact is that most climbers are lithe, flexible, and graceful. If you watch the world's best climbers, you will notice that their climbing is so smooth that it is often difficult to even tell when or where the difficult parts are.

The following basic body positions will begin to teach you how to move and position your body to use not only arm strength, but your entire body to the best of your ability.

The Rule of Opposites

Generally speaking, you will want to always have opposite appendages on the wall. Sound confusing? Let me explain. Ultimately, of course, having both hands and both feet on the wall will be your most stable position—think of Spiderman clinging to a blank wall. This position is great for us mortals, so long as we don't want to move. Problem is, to go up something you eventually have to let go and make progress. In addition, you're going to want to be both pushing with your legs and pulling with your arms for maximum efficiency.

So here's how it should look: If you're stepping with your right leg (i.e., shifting your body weight onto the right foot), you should be pulling with your left arm, and vice versa. Still a little confused? That's understandable, but try this: Keep as much weight on your left foot as possible. Now, pull with your left arm while reaching up for the next hold with your right. Do you feel your body starting to swing out and to the side? This is called a "barn door," and whenever you feel that sensation, it means that something needs to be switched in order to balance your body weight. Step again with your left foot on a hold, but this time pull with your right arm and reach the next hold with your left. Does your body feel more stable and balanced this time? If it does, then congratulations, you're using the rule of opposites!

The Backstep

Figuring out how to reach the next hold is a common problem, especially for women, who are generally shorter than their male counterparts. There are a couple of different ways to use the reach that you have to the best of your ability, the first being by backstepping. (This idea also plays off the rule of opposites.)

The most common way of putting a foot on a hold is to place the big toe/inside of the foot on the hold. While this may feel the most natural, it is often not the most efficient, nor the most effective, way to extend your reach. A backstep means placing the pinkie toe side of your shoe on the hold you are stepping on, and shifting that same hip into the wall. For example, say this is all done with your right foot. This means that you will want to be pulling with your left arm and reaching with your right, creating a long line with your body that is flush to the wall.

Rather than climbing as though going up a ladder, turn your hip into the wall and step with the outside edge of your shoe, giving added height with minimal effort from your arms.

The Drop Knee

The second way of extending your reach is through a move called the "drop knee." Generally speaking (and here again, think of the English language—there is an exception to every rule), climbing is all about tucking your body into the wall. That being said, a drop knee is a very good way of doing just that when, say, your handholds are not very good. The drop knee creates a kind of tripod with your legs, allowing you to lock your body into the wall and push upward.

Drop knees are very helpful in adding height while taking weight off your arms.

The Straight Arm

Remember how I said earlier that you needn't be able to do a single pull-up to climb? Well, that is where climbing straight-armed comes into play. It is a common myth that climbing involves literally pulling your body up the wall. This is not the case at all. It is, in fact, far more efficient to bend your arms as little as possible while climbing, using instead your shoulder, back, and leg muscles, which are all stronger than your biceps. To practice this concept, try climbing a route that is relatively easy without bending your arms. This will force you to use other muscle groups and body positions.

Shake out one arm while the other arm is as straight and relaxed as possible.

One example (of many) of how you can cross one hand over the other to reach the next hold in an energy-efficient way.

All Crossed Up

Imagine this scenario (which can be applied to either hands or feet): There are three holds in a horizontal row. You are holding on to the two leftmost holds and must somehow move directly right to the last of the three. How would you do it? Your first instinct would probably be to somehow switch your hands on the middle hold and then reach right. This would work fine, and is called "matching," but it is not always the most efficient way to progress. Often the best way to conserve energy is by crossing one hand over or under the other, thereby eliminating an extra move in the process.

Unfortunately, as in matters of the heart, our instincts can sometimes lead us astray.

Lean in too close and you might slide off the rock at any minute.

Slabs vs. Overhangs

Unfortunately, as in matters of the heart, our instincts can sometimes lead us astray. When climbing something that is low angle (less than vertical, or "slabby"), it's natural to feel the need to lean in and cling to the wall. Resist the urge! Although it may seem more secure to lean into the wall, the opposite is true. When slab climbing, it's very important to stand straight over your feet. When you lean in on a slab, the weight comes off your feet and this, in turn, will cause your feet to pop off. The more weight you keep centered over your feet, the better they will stick.

The opposite is true when climbing overhanging rock. Your body will instinctively want to hang away from the wall, but this will only make things harder. Keeping your hips tucked into the wall will help you keep the weight over your feet on overhangs.

On overhanging routes, tuck your body tightly into the wall to keep as much weight on your feet as possible.

Centering your body over your feet will give you better friction and stability.

Lead with Your Hips

One of the ways in which women excel at climbing is that we generally have better turnout than men (turnout is the ability to rotate your legs—the movement starts at the hips and causes the knee and foot to turn outward). This is a good thing, because a lot of climbing is momentum-driven. Moving from one hold to the next does not start with the arms. It begins in the feet, of course, but a good deal of force and momentum can be generated through the hips. Having better turnout can help with this concept. Don't let your body get the "droopy drawers" syndrome, with your butt hanging out from the wall. Instead, begin your movement in your hips, generating power that comes up your back, through your shoulders, and *then* out your arms.

Use your hips to push your body up and give additional reach.

This is an example of what not to do.

Shaking Out

While not technically a body position, knowing this trick will save you a lot of effort and sore forearms. When you climb, the blood flows out of your forearms because they are above your head. At the same time, lactic acid enters your forearms because your muscles and tendons are working so hard to keep you on the wall. When this happens, it is called getting "pumped." You can tell when you are very pumped because not only are your forearms slightly swollen and hard to the touch, but you will also find that your fingers magically open up. You literally won't be able to hold on anymore. When you begin to feel this sensation, the proactive move is to rest for a moment by hanging from one arm while letting the other arm dangle at your side. Shake it gently to encourage blood flow back into your arm, then repeat with your other arm.

Lisa stays relaxed despite the angle of the rock. She rests each arm alternately by shaking them below her to return blood flow to the extremities and alleviate her pump.

The High Step

The high step is essentially what it sounds like: You're putting your foot on a high foothold, then rocking your body weight over it until you're basically sitting on your foot. It's also very important to concentrate on pulling with your foot when high-stepping. Imagine curling your toes over, say, a bottle and then trying to pick it off the ground. This is similar to what you want to do with a high step. Wrap your toes around the hold your foot is on, then act as though you're pulling it closer to you. You should feel it in your hamstring because rather than pulling the foothold closer to you, you're pulling your body over the foothold. A high step, if done correctly, can take quite a bit of weight off your arms. You can practice this concept on a very low-angle slab. Put your foot up high on a hold and then try to stand up over it without putting your hands on the wall.

Left to right: 1. To high step, first place your foot on a high hold.
2. Rock your body weight directly over that foot.
3. Then reach for the next hold.

Lisa Hensel cranking through *Go Granny Go*
(V4), Buttermilks, California

The Lock Off

Locking off is what one arm is doing while the other is reaching up for the next hold. When you first begin climbing, your muscles are not trained to lock off, so as you reach up one arm for the next hold, you may feel the other arm begin to lower. To help with this, pull your elbow in close to your body. Rather than clinging to the hold with your bicep strength, try to distribute your weight over your handhold so that it is spread through the muscles of your arm and back.

Tuck your arm tightly into your body to maximize your lock-off potential.

Using Your Feet

It's common when you first begin climbing to think that you need to put your entire foot on every hold, and this is logical: When you're climbing up a ladder, you put the ball of your foot on each rung, which creates the most stable position. When climbing, however, things are different. You are using your feet as an extension of your legs, core, and then upper body. They are to provide stability, but also upward momentum. Even on a very large foothold, if you try to put your entire foot on the hold, it may feel stable, but it's not going to help you move upward. On a very large foothold, don't put everything from heel to toe on the hold. This will pull you down and lock your body position. Just be satisfied with the ball of your foot and toes on the hold. Your shoes have sticky rubber for a reason.

Often when climbing you are going to be standing on a very small edge. In this instance, don't try to put the ball of your foot on the hold. Here you're going to want to use the edge of your shoe, or your big toe. When you do this, you may feel the urge to stand as if on tiptoe, with your heel up. Resist this urge and force your heel down. This will both create better friction for your foot and keep you from getting a condition known as "Elvis leg." (Elvis leg happens when your leg gets very tired. The problem is exacerbated if your heel is high above your toe, because this puts additional strain on your calf muscles.)

Sometimes you will have to "smear" your foot on a wall or slab where there

Rather than putting your foot on as though climbing up a ladder, place it with precision (using the instep of your shoe) on a very small edge.

isn't even a hold. Smearing is going to feel insecure at first, but it can be very helpful in propelling your body in the correct direction or balancing your body while in an awkward position. If you're smearing, you DO want the entire ball of your foot on

Here the heel is up, not only making the foot more likely to slide off but also putting undue stress on the calf muscles, which might result in "Elvis leg."

Forcing your heel down gives you more stability on slabs because more rubber is touching the rock.

the hold. This is because you are relying on the friction between the wall and the rubber on your shoe to keep your foot on. The more shoe rubber you have in contact with the wall, the more likely it is to stick. And again, force your heel down to help keep as much rubber as possible in contact with the rock. Finally, the more weight you place on your foot, the better it will hold. If you try to smear your foot but do not apply any body weight to it, you will not be creating any friction and your foot will slip right off.

. . .

Most importantly, just get out there and have fun. Remember how I said that climbing is one of three activities natural to man? Well, it's true. Listen to your body, and it will teach you how to get up the wall. Watch other women climb and learn from them. Tell your climbing partner when she's doing a move that looks like it might be less awkward if she just shifted her body the other direction. Laugh. Move. Climb. Do you remember what it was like being a kid and climbing up a tree to sit and giggle with your best friend? Well, if you've forgotten, you'll soon remember.

Katie Brown climbing *High Flames Drifter* (5.12c), Virgin River Gorge, Arizona.

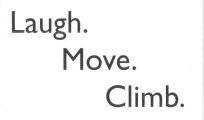

Laugh.
Move.
Climb.

interview

Carol Woods, Amanda's mother (see interview in the previous chapter), is forty-one and works as a behavior coach for a Colorado school district. She has been climbing for five years, since her family encouraged her to try bouldering. After participating in just one competition, she was hooked.

How has climbing impacted your life?
Climbing has taken me out of my comfort zone and helped me explore and examine fears I never thought I had.

How has climbing affected your relationship with your daughter?
Amanda is very supportive of me both inside and out when climbing. She cheers me on and

helps me accomplish the desired climb. We are opposites, so this is a common ground for the two of us.

What do you like about climbing?
I enjoy the social aspect the most when climbing. You do not have to be the best climber to be accepted by the climbing community. Age is not a factor. My children's peers accept me all the way to my peer group.

Do you ever get scared? How do you deal with that?
Climbing terrifies me! I have a crazy fear of heights. When I am stuck on a climb, I pray and God gets me through the worst of it. My family often helps me and encourages me to conquer my fears.

What is your favorite climbing memory together?
My favorite memory of climbing is actually watching my daughter climb. She is an amazing athlete and has so much determination and ability.

What keeps you climbing as a family?
It is incredible how close we are as a family. God is our nucleus and I believe introduced us to this sport so Steve and I could be close to our children. We travel all over the U.S. and world together as a family. What other sport would allow for teens to be cool hanging around their parents all the time?

How do you help motivate or inspire each other?
We inspire each other by encouraging and supporting through our triumphs and failures in climbing.

What's the best thing about having your daughter as a climbing partner?
Amanda is fun to be with on camping trips and just road trips in general. She likes to have fun and see different places. Amanda supports me and is not embarrassed by the fact I compete in the recreational category and only climb V0 to V2. She likes that I try.

Do you think you'll still be climbing in ten years?
I hope to be climbing as long as I can physically. I may never climb any harder than I am now, but that's okay. It's about being with my family and having fun.

> Climbing terrifies me! I have a crazy fear of heights.

Kelley Doyle enjoying a peaceful
evening bouldering session.

Chapter 4

Yes, I get scared. Every day, in fact. I get scared of a lot of things: of traveling alone, of sitting in a restaurant without a dining partner, of what people will think of me—whether I will be good enough, strong enough, successful enough, independent enough, thin enough. The list could go on. And, yes, I am absolutely scared of climbing. Every time I go (which is a lot), I'm scared, and I'd be lying if I said I didn't sometimes question whether or not it's worth it. But I keep going back, just like how every day we continue through life, striving for the things that we love and believe in, in spite of how scary it is.

Growing up, I was painfully shy. Put me in front of a rock wall and I'd think, "Bring it on." Put a microphone in front of my face, however, and I would instantly freeze. My mind would go blank and I couldn't think of a single thing to say. I saw this fear of people and of the spotlight as a flaw in my character, and I hated it. And the more I hated it, the more I withdrew into my shell of shyness. As an adult, however, I discovered that God, Allah, the Big Bang, Buddha, whomever or whatever you may believe in, created some of us outgoing and some of us shy, and that's why the world is balanced. I mean, no one would ever be able to get a word in edgewise if we were all gregarious.

As I became more comfortable with who I was, I found myself able to be more outgoing without even trying. I also discovered as I aged that I excelled at other things, and that I was able to be extroverted in certain situations. For example, put me in a classroom with a prepared speech or something I feel knowledgeable about, or tell me to man a booth at a social event, and I can absolutely be outgoing. But to this day, I continue to struggle if put in a room full of semi-strangers and expected to mingle about, making small talk. Problem is, these kind of events happen all too frequently. Sometimes I'll just not go at all, or I'll bring along an outgoing friend to stick with, or I'll go but make sure to have my own car so I can leave if it gets too uncomfortable. And then, sometimes, I'll make it through an entire evening of mingling without even realizing it. Hopefully, those occasions will come with more regularity as I get older. For now, though, I take what I can get.

I know this may seem like a lengthy divergence from the topic at hand, but bear with me. This is all to say that everyone has fears, and there are important analogies between what I just told you and the important skills that you will learn in this chapter about dealing with your fears.

Zoe Hart spotting for Keri Orton at the Happy Boulders near Bishop, California.

Kelley Doyle bouldering near Bishop, California.

So maybe your fear is of falling or of heights. This doesn't mean that you are flawed, or that you can't or shouldn't try climbing. Courage isn't about not being scared. The most courageous of us all is the one who is absolutely terrified but going for it anyway. I want you to learn to be okay with your fear. It's not a flaw, it's a part of what makes you who you are. Don't avoid the experience of being scared—work with it, not against it. It is my hope that this chapter will help you move in that direction.

Overcoming Fear

There are two things about climbing that generally inspire fear in participants: falling and heights. You will encounter both of these things without a doubt, but let me reiterate that this in no way means that you can't or shouldn't try climbing. Quite the opposite. It means that you should absolutely try climbing, and through it, discover the amazing feeling of overcoming that fear.

Admit You're Scared

First, you must admit that you're scared. Remember how I hated the fact that I was shy? Don't "hate" being scared. It's okay to be scared. Hating that fact about yourself will only cause you to avoid any potential situations where you will encounter the feeling or give others the opportunity to see that part of your character. So start by admitting that you are afraid.

I have spent a lot of time beating myself up for being scared. If you're scared and you forget everything I've told you throughout this chapter, just remember this one thing: Being hard on yourself is definitely not going to help you.

Don't Fight Your Fear

Next, you must learn to be okay with your fear. Don't fight against it or view it as something that you need to "get over." Fact is, fear is something that will never totally dis-appear. I've been climbing for thirteen years, and I'm still scared of falling, as are many of my peers. In addition, being women, we're at somewhat of a disadvantage in the fear department. This isn't to say that our male counterparts aren't scared—they absolutely are, sometimes more than us. However, men, by default, learn to conquer their fears in a way similar to what I'm going to teach you in this chapter. Men are supposed to be brave. It's far more socially acceptable, and sometimes even encouraged, for women to be scared, but a man would more than likely die before letting the girl on the ground watching him know that he is scared.

So, while admitting you're scared may be an easy step, learning to be okay with your fear can be very challenging. This is

Where did the fear come from?

When I was twenty, I realized that I had been climbing, competing, and training for seven years and I no longer loved the sport. I dreaded going climbing, and I finally decided that I needed some time off. That "time off" translated to two years. When I finally got back into climbing, it was a love-hate relationship for some time. I loved it because I found a renewed passion, motivation, and pure enjoyment for climbing. But I also hated it because for some reason I found myself inexplicably scared of falling—so scared, in fact, that I would freeze and be unable to move. I would cry and cry in frustration with myself, not understanding where this paralyzing fear was coming from.

I still don't know where that fear came from. Maybe it was because my skill level was significantly diminished and I no longer felt confident in my ability. Or maybe it was because I was now climbing as an adult and knew the consequences of my actions. I'm not sure. But I'm still climbing, and while I'm still scared, it's not nearly at the level that it was during those first couple years of getting back into climbing. And why is that? Well, it's similar to my story about being shy, so there are some key things that I've learned and want to pass on to you.

because learning to be okay with your fear means doing the opposite of avoiding it. It means stepping up to the plate and trying out this new and exhilarating sport in spite of that admittance of fear.

Confront Your Fear

The third step is to confront your fear. This may sound obvious: Just get out there and climb, right? Well, not exactly. What if your fear is so great that you find yourself unable to even leave the ground? I want to assure you that this is okay, and I'm going to give you several tactics for learning how to confront that inner demon.

Take one move at a time

If you're afraid to leave the ground, start by making a deal with yourself: "Today I will go one move." If that's as far as you can go, so be it. Go up one move. But make another deal with yourself: "Tomorrow I will try and go two moves." Take it as slowly as you need to.

Learn to trust

I know, the rope seems awfully thin when you're staring at it in front of your face and you're far off the ground. Practice learning to trust your equipment and your belayer. Simply tell your belayer to "take," then sit back on the rope until you are completely resting and all four limbs are off the wall. Do this several times throughout a climb, if need be, to remind yourself that the rope is holding you up.

Your climbing partner is your partner because you trust him or her. Try to find someone who you can climb with on a consistent basis. It's important to have a strong climber/belayer relationship, and you will be much more confident if you absolutely trust your belayer.

Practice falling

Don't wait until you're twenty or more feet off the ground and pumped to try falling. Practice some falls while close to the ground to get used to the sensation of being caught by the rope and your partner.

Don't look down

Problem is, you kind of have to look down to see where you need to put your feet next. I mean this more metaphorically. Don't think about what is below you. Focus your energy and attention on the one hold that is in front of you. This goes back to the one-move-at-a-time idea. Don't worry about how far it is to the top, or how high you're going to be once you get there. Give yourself smaller goals, even to the point of them being one move at a time. Once you've completed that goal, create another goal, whether it be the big yellow hold several moves up or simply the next handhold in front of you. Focusing on upward goals will distract your attention from what you're leaving behind (i.e., the ground), and you may find that you're suddenly at the top of the climb without even realizing it.

The author on the *East Face* of Monkey Face (5.12c), Smith Rock, Oregon.

Learn what scares you the most

Learn what scares you the most and what scares you the least. For example, I am not afraid of overhanging climbs, but I am terrified of slab climbing. So if I'm having a scared day, I know that if I search out something overhanging, I'll still have fun. On the other hand, if for whatever reason I'm having a brave day, maybe I'll try a slab to see if I can

get more comfortable on them. It's important to try to tackle that which scares you the most, but don't feel like that's what you have to do every time you go climbing.

Don't be afraid to take a step back

Take things in stages, and don't worry about taking a step back. Like I said above, sometimes you will have brave days and

Brittany Griffith climbing *Cornercopia* (5.10b) in the Lower Gorge at Smith Rock, Oregon.

sometimes you will have scared days, so don't worry if you feel as though you've taken a step back in your progress toward being "brave." Just take things slowly, one day at a time and one move at a time.

Tactics to Combat Fear

It's been my experience that when dealing with fear, it's best to try to start the overcoming process before leaving the ground. Don't wait until you're four feet above a bolt and so scared that you are completely paralyzed before trying out these tactics.

Self-affirmation

Don't be afraid to talk to yourself. Tell yourself before climbing that you are brave, you are strong, and you are safe. Remind yourself verbally that if you do fall, nothing is going to happen. The rope is going to catch you.

Breathe

When you feel yourself beginning to panic, try to consciously focus on your breathing. Deep, slow breaths in and deep, slow breaths out. When we get scared, we tend to start taking short, fast, shallow breaths. This kind of breathing is only going to make you tired faster. Focusing on making sure you're breathing correctly will not only help you calm down psychologically, but will also help you physically.

Assess the Risk

Ask yourself if your fear is reasonable. Sometimes just rationalizing with yourself can help quell your fears.

Visualization

Visualize yourself taking your fear, putting it aside, and leaving it behind. Don't ignore the fear. Look at it straight on and decide that you have the power to overcome it.

Scream

Often, it's not the actual falling that scares us—it's the fear of being out of control or the anticipation of the fall. Have you ever noticed that once you're hanging on the end of a rope, it suddenly doesn't seem that bad? Well, if this is the case, don't be afraid to let out a scream when you fall. Everyone I climb with jokes that I should scream for horror movies because of the blood-curdling yells I often let out upon falling. I find that it's a great release tactic—a way of expelling the fear as I let go.

Step Outside Your Comfort Zone

Don't always accept the toprope. Sometimes it's better to take a step back, but sometimes it's best to suck it up and push yourself. If you don't EVER push yourself, you'll never conquer your fears. If you occasionally force yourself past your level of comfort, eventually you will notice your comfort zone has expanded.

Chick Power

Ever hear of "chick power"? You know, when a guy suddenly finds himself ten times stronger while lifting weights at the gym if a girl is watching? Well, while this may sound a bit superficial, don't be afraid to use the desire to impress those watching you to your advantage.

Lisa Hensel climbing
Mad Dog (5.11+),
Indian Creek, Utah.

Tough Love

Take the word *take* from your vocabulary. Sometimes the answer to combating your fear is to get a bit of tough love from your climbing partner. Tell your partner that you are no longer going to say "take" but are instead going to climb until you fall. Tell her you want her to encourage you to continue climbing even when you feel scared and want to hang on the rope rather than falling.

Work through Fatigue

Use bouldering as a tool to work through your pump. It's common to get more scared when you're tired. However, if you get comfortable climbing through your fatigue while close to the ground, when you're on the real thing, you will be more familiar with the feeling and it will be easier to deal with.

Climb Dynamically

You can also use bouldering as a tool to learn to climb dynamically. Again, it's easy to get more scared when faced with a situation where you are forced to lunge, move dynamically, or even dyno (where all points of contact leave the wall as you jump up to catch a hold that is otherwise out of reach). This is because these kind of moves are known as "low percentage" moves. This means that the percentage of times you are going to successfully make, or "stick," this move is lower than a static move. Also, climbing dynamically often elicits a feeling of losing control. Obviously, particularly when you are high off the ground, a lot of fear stems from the idea of losing control. That being said, if you practice climbing dynamically while close to the ground, you will both improve your ability to stick dynamic moves and get more comfortable with the feeling of being out of control in a safe environment.

Lead Climbing

A lot of new climbers experience a significant jump in their fear level when they begin lead climbing. This is understandable, because when leading, you are clipping a piece of protection and then climbing above it. This means that you are going to be forced to fall the distance to your last piece of protection and then that same distance below it before you stop. While this can be a frightening proposition, learning to lead climb can also be an exhilarating experience.

To begin the process toward lead climbing, I recommend mock leading. Set up a toprope, and then tie into a second rope. This way you can learn the feeling of leading, of having the rope below you instead of above you, and of clipping—all without having the added challenge of overcoming the fear factor at the same time.

It will also help to practice falling while mock leading. This will require two belayers: One person will belay you on toprope and the other will belay you on lead. (This is also a good way to teach people how to lead belay, but for starters, make sure your lead belayer is an experienced one, as it is a skill in and of itself.) Your toprope belayer is going to keep a large loop of slack in the rope but will be there to act as both a backup safety and a security blanket. Start by going one move above your bolt, then two, then three, then as far as you are comfortable.

Once you're confident mock leading, move on to the real thing. As I said before, if this is overwhelmingly frightening, don't be afraid to start slow. Go one bolt at a time if needed, hanging and resting on each one as you go. If you need to, just go a few moves above your bolt and then downclimb back down to the bolt. Eventually, however, it's important to start falling. I know this is scary, so remember what I talked about above.

Following are some things to remember to make lead falls an enjoyable experience.

Fall Like a Cat

When you fall on toprope, but more importantly on lead, it's crucial to stay alert to where you are "landing." When I fall, I usually grab my knot with both hands. It makes me feel more secure, plus it gives me something to hold on to while I'm sailing through the air. Also, don't let your body go completely floppy. Keep your body taut and your legs slightly apart and ready to land—like a cat. See page 19 for a good photo of this technique.

Beware of Your Rope

One of the most important things to remember while climbing is to avoid putting the rope behind your leg. The rope should always be between your leg and the rock.

This is because if the rope goes behind your leg and you fall, the rope has the potential to flip you upside down at worst, or give you a rope burn at best.

Back-Clipping

When you clip your rope into the quickdraw, the rope should run up the rock and out to you. If the rope is running the opposite direction, it has the possibility of unclipping itself when you fall.

Lead Belaying

Lead belaying is an important skill, and if learned correctly can save a new climber from a lot of unpleasantness. The most common mistake in lead belaying is keeping the rope too tight. It's our natural response when someone falls to take in as much slack as possible, and this is true for toproping. For leading, however, if the rope is too tight, when you fall it is going to swing you back into the rock and cause you to "land" with far more force than desired. You might get hurt, and even if you don't, slamming into the rock when you fall is never fun.

Having said that, the belayer should keep a small loop of slack in the rope. If the climber is heavier than the belayer, that's all the belayer needs to do. Should the climber be a weight similar to or lighter than the belayer, however, it's important for the belayer to jump in the air when the climber is falling. This is going to give what is called a "dynamic" fall. When the climber falls, she is shock-loading the rope and her gear, and having the belayer jump is going to eliminate a large part of that shock, making it so that the climber not only avoids the wall when she falls, but also lands as though on a pile of pillows.

• • •

There's a line in a reggae song that I heard once that says, "Use what you've got to get what you want." All things aside, if you forget every trick I've given you in this chapter to help deal with fear, just remember one thing: Don't be afraid of your fear. Just use what you have to get what you want.

Don't be afraid of your fear.

interview

Lauren Lee is a twenty-seven-year-old student and climber who lives in St. George, Utah, but is originally from Cincinnati, Ohio. She has been climbing for more than eight years, and while she started climbing indoors, she now spends the majority of her time bouldering and sport climbing outdoors. Having a fear of falling is something that Lauren has greatly struggled with over the years, but her love for the movement and challenge of climbing has kept her in the sport and helped her find ways to cope with and overcome her fear.

I heard that you used to be really scared of falling. How did you overcome that fear?

You heard correct. Falling for me has been a traumatic experience. It could stem from the natural inclination to remain safely within perimeters that don't challenge gravity, but it could also stem from a sport-climbing accident I had while belaying Liv Sansoz. Human error is possible, and knowing this firsthand certainly made me more aware of the need for safety.

Both of the above issues, however, have been individual issues that arise when I find myself on the sharp end of the rope. I honestly can't say that I have overcome my fear of falling, but I have formulated an analytical system that allows me to manage the fear. The first thing that I do when I'm overcome with fear is to analyze the situation. To break it down: First, I allow myself to realize that my fears are generally irrational. Next, I try to talk myself through the fear, or open up a dialog with my belayer. Most of the time, I end up laughing at my self-inflicted fear, which in turn makes me feel relaxed so that I can keep on climbing.

Lauren Lee on *Mr. Choad's Wild Ride* (5.11b), Red Rocks, Nevada.

Can you describe what it feels like when you get scared? What usually brings it on?

Fear has a spectrum of emotions, so it's hard to distinguish one from the other, especially when you are in the middle of it. First, though, I usually get a mental image that triggers a panic mode—a textbook example of anxiety. The mental image is usually the thought of a scary fall, or of not believing myself able to get to the next hold. From there, I think the reaction between my mind and body starts shutting down, restricting the flow of oxygen to the muscles. My forearms feel fatigued to the point that I can't even imagine holding on. That's usually when I yell for my belayer to take, and I end up feeling demoralized for not trying hard.

What other fears within climbing do you deal with?

As I mentioned earlier, my accident with Liv made me afraid to belay. It took a lot of confidence and persistence from friends to get me to climb again. I took the accident as a clear sign that I was inexperienced. In order to keep my climbing buddies and myself safe, I accepted all criticism and I focused on safety. I have a routine where I always check my knot and belay device. It allows me to stay calm, knowing that all the safety devices are correctly in place. Staying calm is imperative for success in climbing, whether that be as a climber or belayer.

What strengths do you think climbing has given you?

Climbing has strengthened my bond with the great outdoors. Climbing for the sheer joy of being present has taught me that showing up is the start to something bigger.

How has climbing impacted/changed your life?

Climbing has been a learning tool and a connection to a distant life that I once led. It has been a good example of how practical application results in higher learning and expertise. Climbing rounds me out and keeps me working on new challenges.

More than anything I like the places that climbing takes me . . .

What do you like about climbing?
More than anything I like the places that climbing takes me, from the old familiar favorites to the distant lands of new adventure.

What advice would you give other women who are interested in the sport but intimidated?
The best advice I can give to women who have interest in climbing is to find a friend and get to a gym or a clinic. Find an environment that makes you feel open to new learning experiences. Oh! And enjoy . . .

story

A Lesson in Fear

The most scared I've ever been while climbing was on a 5.6 slab in Zion National Park. I can see the quizzical look on your face right now as you read this. Yes, I am a professional climber, and 5.6 *should* be far below my climbing ability. And it is—usually. But when it comes to frightening situations in climbing, difficulty doesn't always equal scary.

It was my first climbing trip with another girl—just the two of us, heading to Zion in my beat-up van to learn how to aid climb. It felt somehow liberating and yet intimidating at the same time to know that there was no guy to bail us out in a bad situation. Being the stronger free climber, I felt pressure to be brave and bold—to lead our little team. My partner, Jen, however, was the far more experienced aid climber, so I'm sure she felt pressure as well to teach me the tricks of the trade and to be in charge of that side of our climb.

On our first day of climbing, we made it three pitches up a nine-pitch route that we had originally planned on doing in a day. The day was a comedy of errors and mishaps, mainly as I struggled with the concept of aid climbing and trusting in my gear when every fiber of my being screamed to put my hands and feet in the crack instead. My partner discovered that she had a new food allergy

Katie Brown grappling with fear on *Miss Kitty Likes It That Way* (5.11d), Maverick Buttress, Moab, Utah.

and spent the majority of the day scratching her arms and legs and yelling aid-climbing advice up to me.

On our second day, however, things seemed to go a bit smoother. I reverted to free climbing and moved more quickly, and we thought everything was going exceedingly well as we neared the final pitch to success late in the afternoon. We stood on a huge ledge and peered up at the last, slabby bulge that prevented us from standing on top in victory. The topo was a bit unclear as to where to go exactly, but it was supposed to be 5.6, so I figured I could just scamper to the summit any which way.

Up I headed, clipping two bolts and then stepping onto another huge ledge. From here, things looked even more confusing. There was a gully to my left and a slab in front of me. The gully seemed unlikely, so I started straight up the slab. My plan of "scampering" to the top soon came to a screeching halt. The rock was impossibly soft and granular, eroding away beneath my hands and feet. I tried to brush off the sloping undulations that were to be my footholds and handholds,

> I crouched down on the ramp and tried to slow my breathing. I knew I couldn't sit there forever. I yelled down to my partner in a quavering voice, "I don't know what to do . . ."

but this only presented me with more sand. Nonetheless, I continued up. Gear was non-existent, but I searched and searched and finally found a yellow Alien that just barely slid into a sandy, flaring pseudo-crack. The piece would pull out for sure if I fell, but I was hoping it would provide enough moral support to get me to the top.

Pretty soon I encountered a large sloping ramp, and nothing else for hands and feet. It looked like maybe, just maybe, there were going to be good handholds up above, if I could just get my feet up to this ramp. Problem was, I would have to mantle the ramp and that might put me in a situation where I could no longer reverse the moves I had done thus far.

I looked down and looked up and contemplated my options in the dwindling daylight. Jen must have been down below wondering what on earth was taking me so long. We had to get to the top to reach the descent trail; otherwise, we'd have to rappel the route on our one lead line and six-millimeter tag line. So up I went, mantling onto this incredibly sandy, incredibly scary, sloping ramp.

As soon as I stood up on the ramp and felt the ridges that I thought were going to be my saving grace, I knew I was f*%$ed. Nothing, no holds anywhere, and no gear. And to top it off, the rock quality was disintegrating with alarming speed. I looked down at the one, poor piece of gear that separated me from the ledge below. I tried to calculate where I would land if the piece blew: It would *maybe* keep me from hitting the ledge. If the piece did blow, however, I would undoubtedly go careening straight into the ledge. I pictured myself landing on an ugly tree stump that somehow managed to protrude from a crack in the ledge, getting knocked unconscious, and then rolling off the ledge, leaving me dangling from the bolt I had clipped early on in the pitch and within sight of my partner.

Being a writer, I have a slightly overactive imagination. It began to get the best of me, and my breath started coming in short, desperate gasps. I could either try to reverse the move (which elicited an image in my mind of slipping off the sandy ramp with my foot above my head—never a good way to fall), or I could try to continue on up, thereby risking the possibility of making my situation even worse.

I crouched down on the ramp and tried to slow my breathing. I knew I couldn't sit there forever. I yelled down to my partner in a quavering voice, "I don't know what to do . . ."

She hollered up in response, "Ummm, okay. What's going on?" I explained the situation to her, unsure of what she could hear and what she was missing. "Well, ummm, I don't know what to tell you," she replied.

For some reason, I had hoped she was going to give me some magic solution, something along the lines of, "This is how you will reverse your moves, and then I will come up and finish the pitch for you." No such luck. I felt like crying. Oh wait, I was crying.

I sat there ruminating and mumbling to myself: "Why do I always have to be the stronger climber, the one who has to lead and be brave? Sometimes I just want to be the girl and be taken care of . . . it's so not fair."

Clearly, self-pity was getting me nowhere in this situation, and the sun was rapidly setting. I felt locked in fear and indecision, unable to move one way or another. But only I could fix this situation, no one else, and something had to be done. Finally, I yelled down, "Okay, I'm going to try to reverse this mantle. It would be bad if I fell, so wish me luck. If all goes well and I get down, we're going to have to rappel the route."

"Okay," Jen yelled back up. She sounded as nervous as me. I'm sure not being able to see what I had gotten myself into wasn't helping. Down I went, my breath raspy with fear and little prayers slipping from my lips. My fingers turned white as I gripped the sandy ramp, and they started slipping just as I lowered my toes far enough to rest on something I could stand on.

"Okay! I'm good!" I yelled down in jubilation. I had done it. I scrambled carefully back down to the ledge, taking the yellow Alien out without even having to pull the trigger. I then slipped over the next edge and downclimbed the bolted portion of the route, coming to rest next to my partner at the belay.

I was mortified, completely and totally embarrassed. I had failed our team, and now it was almost dark. Things were quiet as we readied to rappel. Jen took a look at our six-millimeter tag line and broached the question, "Did you check to see if this thing is rated for body weight?"

Again, embarrassment filled me. Here I was, the "pro," and I hadn't even thought about something as simple as making sure we'd be able to bail in an emergency. Clearly, all my whining to myself up above about wanting to be "taken care of" was completely unfounded. Obviously, the problem was that I had been taken care of *too much* in the past, and now I was unprepared to be out climbing with a peer rather than someone who wasn't my superior in skill and experience.

"I have no idea if it is or not. I'm really sorry," I muttered.

Jen, having more aid-climbing and guiding experience, breathed in deeply and took charge. "Okay, well, we don't have any choice, so we'll just have to hope. I'll back it up on the first rappel and you'll go first. Then I'll undo the backup and come down after."

I nodded silently. I was so humbled, and I felt completely ridiculous. Down we went in this manner, in the pitch black, and one rappel after another the tiny tag line continued to hold us.

I was sure, as our feet finally hit terra firma late in the night, that Jen would never talk to me again, let alone climb with me. At the same time, though, I was excited that I had conquered my fear and at least *acted*—that I had done something in a situation where there was no one there, no boy who was stronger than me to bail me out. I felt embarrassed and yet empowered with the knowledge that there was so much I needed to learn, experience, and conquer.

Since that road trip, I have learned so much about climbing and being prepared, and I approach every situation with a certain humility and respect for the partner, male or female, that I may be climbing with.

Being in that situation also taught me something important about fear. That moment was the first time in my life where I was scared for a reason and not simply because I was just plain afraid. The situation really was a dangerous one, where one wrong move meant that I would probably get seriously hurt. And yet despite the very real danger I had put myself in front of, I discovered that I could overcome my fear—I could take control of it, harness it, and use it to my advantage. I hadn't had a choice but to conquer my fear. I had nowhere to turn, and in turn I was empowered with the knowledge of what I could accomplish in those many situations where I did have a choice.

So often we are afraid when there is nothing to be afraid of—when our rational minds can analyze the situation and tell us that we're safe, but we are still paralyzed with fear. It's a situation that you do have power over, and as hard as it feels to step over that line into the scary "out-of-my-comfort-zone" place, it is doable, and it is worth it.

The author having fun again on *Swedin-Ringle* (5.12), Indian Creek, Utah.

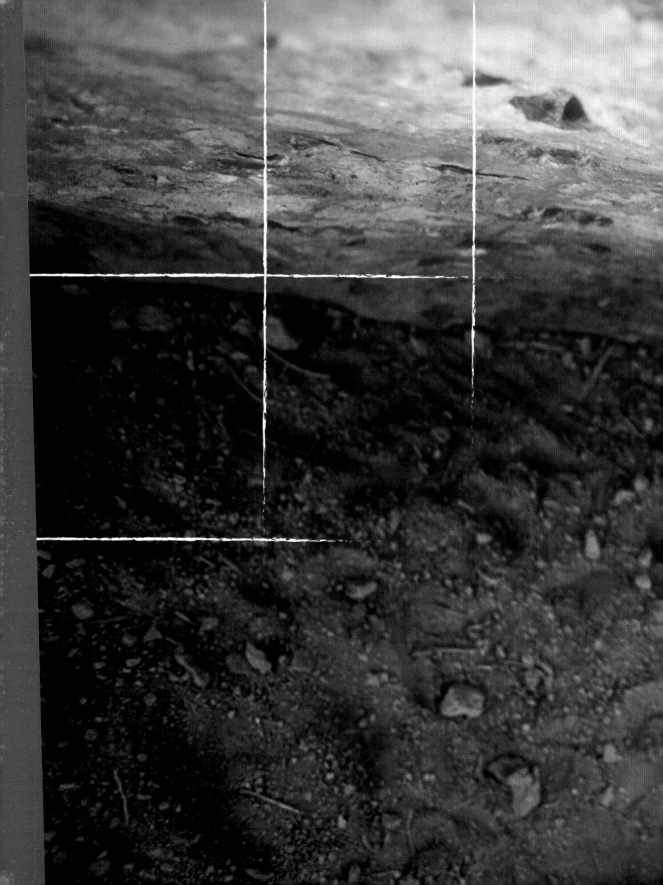

Chapter 5

Marie-Andree Cloutier bouldering *Groundwater* (V5) at the Happy Boulders, California.

Lisa Hensel racking up at
Indian Creek, Utah.

While there are many different genres of climbing, in this book we are going to focus on sport climbing, bouldering, and traditional climbing. These are not only the more popular variations of the sport, but are also the most common way to be introduced to climbing.

- In sport climbing all the protection is pre-placed, usually in the form of bolts. You will need a rope, a dozen or so quickdraws, shoes, a harness, a chalk bag, and a belay/rappel device.

Sport climbing gear.

- Bouldering is ropeless climbing that involves doing difficult moves relatively low to the ground. For bouldering you will need shoes, a chalk bag, and a crash pad.

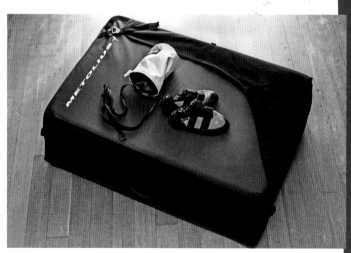

Bouldering gear.

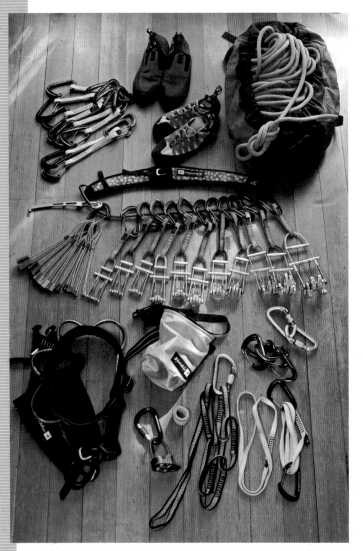

Trad climbing gear.

• Traditional climbing (trad climbing) requires a climber to place most or all protection points and belay anchors in the rock, usually in the form of removable devices such as nuts and cams. For traditional climbing you will need a set of cams (preferably two of each size to start with), a set of stoppers, several quickdraws, several long runners, a couple of extra locking carabiners, shoes, a harness, a chalk bag, and a belay/rappel device.

Techniques for Sport Climbing and Bouldering

For both sport climbing and bouldering, the basic body positions that I explained in chapter 3 will provide a solid basis of technique on which to start. There are, however, some specific techniques and movements that will come in handy. The longer you climb, the deeper your pool of techniques to draw upon will be, but when you first begin, it may not occur to you to try taking a handhold in a certain manner. Plus, it never hurts to learn some climbing jargon so you will know what your fellow climbers are talking about!

The techniques described here mostly apply to face climbing as opposed to crack climbing (described in the upcoming section on traditional climbing). Face climbing is what you usually will be doing when sport climbing and bouldering.

Crimping vs. Open-Handing

Most climbers tend to go one way or the other when it comes to how they prefer to "take" a hold. For example, I will crimp just about everything because that is how I am stronger, but I have friends who rarely crimp because their hands are stronger in an open-handed position. Experiment with both to determine which way your feel stronger. There are certain holds, however, that are going to be better to grab one way or the other across the board.

Crimping a crimper

Duh, right? You crimp a crimper. A crimper is any hold that is very narrow—one that does not protrude from the wall much. Sometimes you'll only be able to get half a pad of your finger on the hold. To get the best purchase on these holds, you're going to curl your fingers up and bring your thumb over top the other fingers. Wrapping your thumb around your fingers will give you additional strength because you'll be able to pull with all five of your digits instead of just four.

A crimp is a small but usually positive hold. Generally speaking, you will gain the most power from a crimp by curling your fingers around it.

Using your thumb to push down on your fingers can increase holding power on a crimp.

A sloper is a large, rounded hold. Friction helps you hold slopers, so the more of your hand that is making contact with the rock, the better.

A side pull is vertically aligned rather than horizontally. Take the hold and pull on it sideways toward your body.

Open-handing a sloper

Slopers are large, bulbous holds with little on them that is "positive" (something you can really dig your fingers into). I must confess that I will often try to crimp even slopers, but if you can train your body to grab these holds open-handed, you will be stronger in the long run. To do this, you're going to want to get as much surface area onto the hold as possible. The more surface area, the more friction you will have. This means that your hand will be in an open position so that not only are your fingertips touching the hold, but so are all of your fingers, the palm of your hand, and on very large slopers, even your forearm.

Side Pull vs. Gaston

Holds that are vertical in orientation are often overlooked because it is our natural inclination to think that we can only grab those holds that are horizontal, like a pull-up bar. Vertical holds can be quite useful, however, if you know how to grab them correctly.

The side pull

A side pull is a vertical hold that you are going to grab with your fingertips facing toward you. Rather than trying to pull down on it, you are going to lean out on it and step up (often with a backstep to create the ideal body positioning) and lever your body upward. Obviously, every move is different, but this movement will often be done with a straight arm and your back muscles doing the most work.

The gaston

A gaston is a hold that you will grab with your fingertips facing away from you and your elbow out. Using gastons is quite awkward at first, so don't be surprised if it feels odd to have your hand facing the "wrong" direction.

Bumping

It's a common misconception that climbing is similar to crawling: right, left, right, left. It may go that way sometimes, but it's important to remember that there are other options. In chapter 3 I covered the option of matching on holds, or crossing to maximize efficiency, but there is also a technique called "bumping." Sometimes you will encounter holds that are just good enough to hold on to, but not good enough to move off. In this position, it's wise to stop and assess what hold is coming next. Simply because you've just moved your left hand up doesn't mean that you must now move your right. Maybe the hold you've moved your left hand to is very bad, but the next one coming up looks really good. Well, "bump" again with your left hand to the better hold before trying to move your right. These holds that are somewhere between good and completely unusable are called "intermediates" and are very useful for making long moves, pausing to adjust your feet, or helping you generate a little extra momentum.

A gaston is a vertically aligned hold facing the opposite direction of a side pull. To use one, put downward and outward force on the hold to push your body in the intended direction.

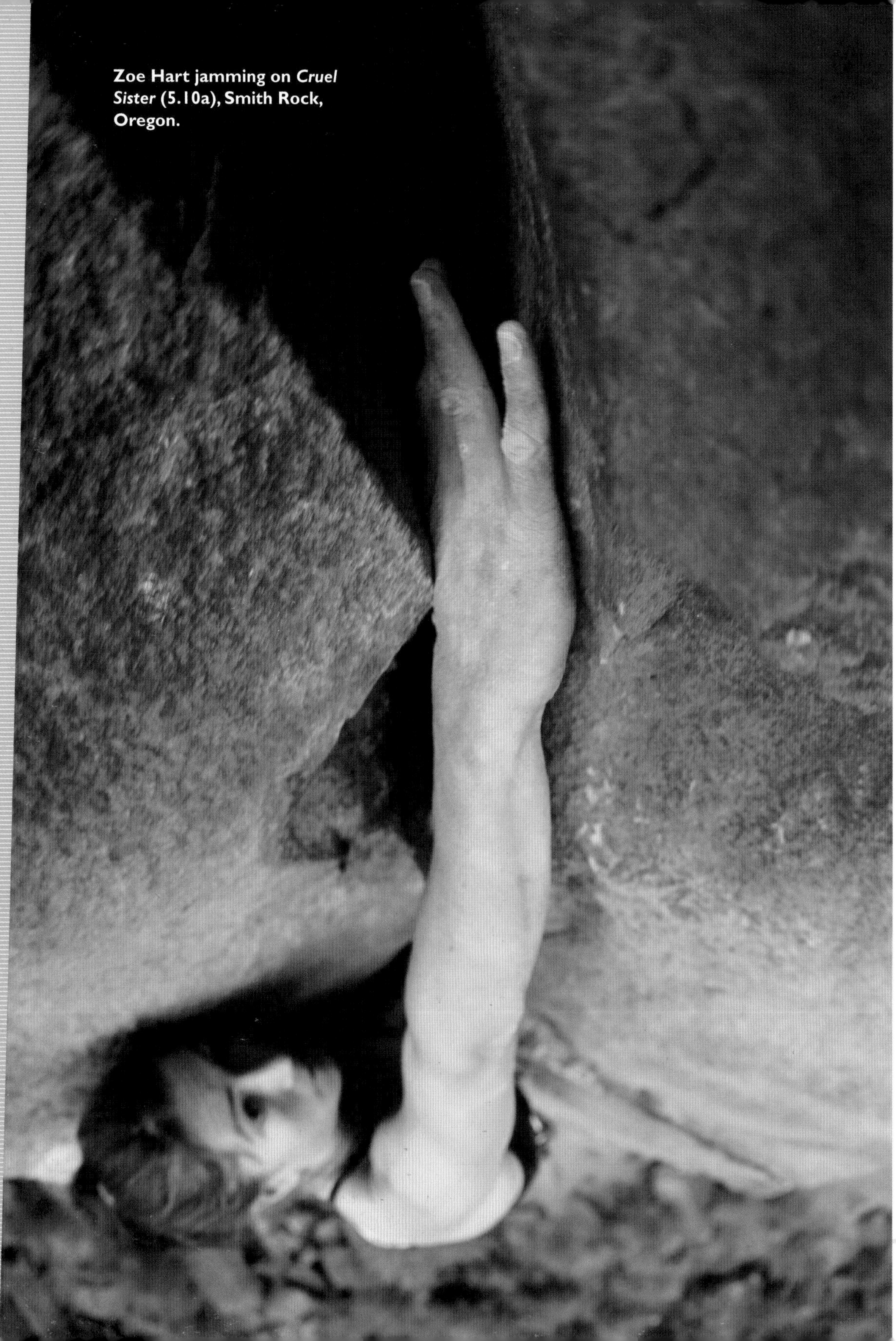

Zoe Hart jamming on *Cruel Sister* (5.10a), Smith Rock, Oregon.

Techniques for Traditional Climbing

If you decide to take up traditional climbing (also called trad climbing), there is a whole different set of techniques that you will need to learn in addition to those described above. It's called "traditional" because it is the original way that climbing began, when there was no such thing as bolts that could be drilled into the rock and left there. Consequently, people began creating protection devices that would lodge into the rock (usually into cracks), catching them if they fell but still removable upon completing a climb. Because traditional climbing is generally centered around cracks and cracks cannot be "grabbed" in the same way that a hold protruding from a face can be held, there is a whole series of techniques specifically for crack climbing.

The Hand Jam

To hand jam, slide your hand into the crack, flattening it to make it as thin as possible. Then cup your hand, pulling your thumb in and down as you do and flexing your thumb muscle. The crack should be touching the back of your hand on one side and your thumb muscle on the other. If your thumb muscle gets pumped as you climb, you are doing it right. It may take some experimenting, but once you get the technique down, a hand jam should feel so solid that it seems like you will never fall out of it.

Flexing your thumb muscle widens your hand and creates a constriction, "locking" the hand between the two walls of the crack.

A hand jam can be placed thumbs up or thumbs down (as pictured here).

The Finger Lock

Slide your fingers into the crack, pointer finger down, then rotate your elbow directly in line with the crack. This will lock your fingers into the crack. Often (and this is also true with hand jamming) your top hand will be pointer finger down and your lower hand will be pinkie down. This is not a steadfast rule, however, so if that position doesn't feel right, try something different, such as having both hands with pointer fingers down.

The same can be done with the pinky down, especially if the crack is too small for the pointer finger.

When doing a finger lock, slot your fingers into the crack and then pull your elbow down parallel to the crack.

The Ring Lock

There are two sizes that just about every climber, regardless of experience, struggles with. These are the ring lock and the finger stack, and both fall somewhere between finger locks and hand jams. Ring locks are used when the crack is slightly too big to get a solid finger lock. To ring lock, put your fingers in as if you were going to finger lock, but then curl your pointer finger down, making the meat of your first digit as fat as possible. Next, hook your thumb over your pointer finger, locking it into place. The meat of your pointer finger is what is going to lock into the crack.

To use a ring lock make an "OK" sign with your index finger and thumb and slot the ring into the crack, tightening it to make your finger as fat as possible. This will lock the meat of your pointer finger between the walls of the crack. Pull your elbow down parallel to the crack as you would with a standard finger lock.

The Finger Stack

Even worse than the ring lock is the finger stack. This awkward size is the nemesis for many a climber, so don't feel bad if you find yourself shying away from cracks of this size as you learn. Again, slide your fingers into the crack, pointer down. Place your thumb behind your fingers, then rotate your elbow in, as if you were finger locking. You essentially are, except that your thumb is acting as an additional spacer between your fingers and the crack. When crack climbing, it is generally advisable to keep your hands closer to your face, but for this technique I find it works better if my top hand is as high above me as possible.

When doing a finger stack, your thumb goes between your finger and the wall of the crack, thereby widening your hand to fit. Again, be sure to pull the elbow down and parallel to the crack to lock the fingers.

The Fist Jam

Once the crack widens past hand jams, you are again going to have to employ different techniques to get your hands to fit, starting with the fist jam, which is simple. Make a fist and slide it into the crack. Generally speaking, your top hand should have your knuckles facing you, while your bottom hand should have your fingers pointed in your direction.

When doing fist jams your bottom fist usually jams with fingers facing you, while the upper fist has fingers facing away from you. Shuffle hands in this manner to move upward.

Make a fist and squeeze it to engage the hand muscles.

Offwidths

There are several different techniques used for offwidths, which are cracks that are too wide for your hands but not wide enough to fit your whole body in, or "chimney." Offwidth climbing involves a great deal of patience, creativity, and all-out groveling. Some people love it and others hate it. Refer to the photos to learn several techniques useful for getting up an offwidth—they are much easier to show than describe.

The more you bend your leg in an offwidth, the wider the leg will get and the better it will stay in the crack. Keep your foot outside the crack (a technique commonly called "froggie foot") to hold your leg in place and keep your balance.

A standard arm bar. Create pressure between your hand and triceps to lock yourself into the crack.

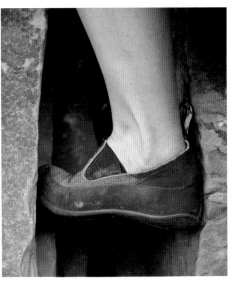

This is a common foot technique used in wide cracks. Your entire foot creates a camming action inside the crack.

The hand stack is a technique used when the crack is too wide for one hand and both hands must be used. Any combination of two hands jams, a hand and fist, or two fist jams can be used, depending on the size of the crack. To move your hands you can either use your shoulder to hold you in place while sliding your hands upward, or you can use a leg bar to do the same.

An example of fist stacks.

Footwork

With the exception of offwidths, foot placement is generally the same for all of the techniques above, regardless of the size of the crack. Slide your foot, pinkie toe down, into the crack. The key here is to not so much stick the toe of your shoe in, but rather the entire back edge of your shoe. Once your foot is slotted, rotate your knee so that it is in line with the crack. This will cam your foot into the crack as you step up.

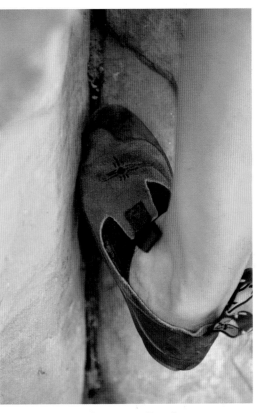

When the crack is too small to fit your foot, put as much in as possible and use essentially the same camming technique as with a bigger crack. Keep as much shoe rubber as possible in contact with the rock to create better friction.

Slot your foot pinky toe down into the crack. Then, as you step up on it, it will rotate in the crack and create a camming action.

Lead Climbing

In addition to climbing techniques, you are going to need to learn how to place and clip gear. When you begin climbing, you will start out toproping, which means that the rope will be taken to the top of the route by a lead climber and then secured there for you. Once you begin leading, however, you will need to learn how to attach (or "hang") quickdraws to the bolts in the rock—or place traditional gear—and then clip your rope into the quickdraws.

When sport climbing, the number of quickdraws you carry should correspond to the number of bolts on your climb, plus two for the anchor. You will simply attach one draw to each bolt and then clip your rope into it as you climb. Figuring out how to clip your rope into the quickdraw with one hand can sometimes be tricky, so the photos will give you some tips on how to clip. For sport climbing, you will also need to learn how to "clean" the route you climbed. Cleaning is the act of safely retrieving the quickdraws that you've placed on the route. This process can be tricky on steep routes or routes that don't follow a straight line, and the techniques are best learned through classes, clinics, or at your local gym.

When you first begin leading on tradi-

If the gate is facing away, place your thumb on the back of the carabiner like this. Use the opposing pressure of your thumb against your fingers to push the gate open and slide the rope in.

If the gate is facing you, place your middle finger inside the carabiner like this and pull on it. Hold the rope between your thumb and index finger, then push the rope through the gate.

tional gear, it is very important to have an experienced traditional climber with you—somebody who can climb the route after you, check your gear, and give you constructive criticism. For starters, though, I will give you a basic idea of how to appropriately place gear. Again, for in-depth instruction on anchor building, cleaning, multi-pitch climbing, and other aspects of traditional climbing, it is best to learn in person.

Cams

When placing a cam, you want to be sure that all of the lobes are coming into contact with the rock. You also want to make sure that the cam is neither under-cammed in too wide a crack (the unit might "walk" itself out of the crack), nor over-cammed in too small a crack (you might never get it out).

This solid cam placement has good contact and a range of retraction of about 50 percent.

Over-cammed units like this might never come out. A smaller cam is needed for this crack.

Never place a unit with the cams loosely "tipped out" like this. A bigger cam is needed.

Stoppers

Stoppers are passive camming devices that are placed into constrictions in the rock. A stopper should wedge into a constriction like a puzzle piece.

A solid nut placement maintains good contact with the rock and slots nicely into a constriction.

Nuts can also be placed on their minor axis like this.

This poor nut placement maintains minimal contact with the rock and should not be trusted.

Similar to climbing on a rope, it is important to "fall like a cat" when bouldering. Stay relaxed so that your spotter may assist you but be aware of where you are falling.

The ideal spotting stance. Keep your gaze focused on the climber's hips.

Spotting

Bouldering is a bit different from sport and traditional climbing because you will not be using a rope. You will be falling on a crash pad, and your climbing partner will be "spotting" you. It is important to both spot and fall correctly. When placing crash pads below a climber, make sure that the pads are overlapping one another so that there is no opportunity for the climber's foot to fall in between the pads. Also, if spotting someone who is traversing, be sure to drag the pad accordingly so that it is always centered below her.

If you are the climber, the most important thing you can do is to be aware when you are falling. Don't just go limp when you fall and expect your spotter to catch you.

That's why they're called "spotters" and not "catchers." The key is to fall like a cat, not like a bag of sand. You're going to hit the ground, so just be prepared. Luckily, there's a nice, soft crash pad to protect you.

If you are the spotter, your main job is to protect the climber's head, or try to right her body if she is falling at a strange angle. To spot, position yourself below and a step or two behind the climber. Hold your arms out with your thumbs tucked, and track the climber's waist with your eyes. You should not be watching the climber's limbs, but rather her core. When she falls, your hands should be at about her rib cage. What you are trying to do is help guide her body to the crash pad.

Rules for a Sport with No Rules

Most climbing etiquette revolves around common sense. Be kind and courteous to people you are climbing around. If you're climbing outdoors, check with those around you before doing something that may bother them, like playing loud music. Stay on the trail and pack out any garbage.

Here are a few more fundamental etiquette rules that are a good idea to follow:

• Don't spend too long on a climb. If you are climbing in a busy gym or at a popular crag, try to understand that other people might want to do the route you're on.

• If there is a line for a climb, it'll often be marked by someone leaving their rope at the base of the climb. Look out for this or some other marker so as to avoid snaking someone's turn.

• Wipe away your tick marks. Tick marks are large streaks made by chalk on the rock that climbers will often leave to help them remember where to grab certain holds. This is acceptable but can be unsightly, so when you are done, wipe away your marks.

• If there are quickdraws left on a route overnight, this is because a person plans to come back and try that particular route again. Don't take the quickdraws.

• Don't be rude to your belayer or argue with your belayer at the crag. Obviously, you're sometimes going to have disagreements with your climbing

Joi Gallant sliding in a cam so she doesn't have to use one of her _Nine Lives_ (5.11+), Indian Creek, Utah.

partners, but try to be respectful of those around you so they can have an enjoyable time as well.

• Sometimes when climbers are trying to redpoint a route, they can be particular about the sort of encouragement they get. Ask them if they like encouragement or if loud encouragement distracts them.

interview

Lara Antonelli is a thirty-four-year-old physician's assistant in Moab, Utah. She has been climbing for four and a half years.

Lara Antonelli at Hueco Tanks, Texas.

What is it that you like about climbing?
I don't have to use my legs. [Laugh.] No, that's actually my problem with climbing—I need to use my legs better. I like climbing because I like the environment of the sport. For example, in Washington state you're climbing in beautiful forests, and in the desert you're climbing while surrounded by stunning red rock.

Why did you choose climbing instead of some other sport?
Well, I can't really say that I consciously "chose" climbing. I was exposed to it by someone that I was dating, and I enjoyed it so . . . I kept doing it. It's not like I researched climbing and then made a conscientious decision to pursue it. But why am I still doing it? It's fun, it's social, it's a great environment, and it's a full body workout.

How do you juggle your career with recreating outdoors?
Well, it wasn't for climbing per se, but I definitely chose a career that allows me the luxury of having some flexibility in my schedule. I think, though, that if I did work eight-to-five, five days a week, I would still make it a priority to climb on weekends. It's just that I'm lucky that the type of work I do affords me that luxury—which was one of my goals in choosing that line of work.

Why do you like climbing with other women?
I think women are much more positive and supportive. I think that it's much more fun and that women tend to go climbing for better reasons, whereas with men I see a lot of ego building and "dude-ish" behavior, like chest butting and chest thrusting to see who can climb harder. Also, men seem to have goals and if they don't meet them, they tend to throw temper tantrums—but I have never in my life seen a female climber throw a temper tantrum. I've seen tears, hurt feelings, and frustration, but I've never seen a woman come off a climb and throw a childish temper tantrum. And, unfortunately, it seems as though some men are predisposed to that.

When you are climbing with both men and women, there seems to be this certain level of machismo. Maybe it's an unconscious condescension toward women climbers in general, but I find that if you climb around women, you walk away feeling like you had a better experience. I feel like I've only really started to improve in climbing since I've started climbing almost exclusively with women.

What has climbing "given" you?
Climbing, for me, is about little goals, because no matter what you do, there's always something harder and there's always something easier. It's fun to complete your goals, which is always exciting. And then as you continue to progress, you can look back at how far you've come. It really puts things in perspective, and you can apply that to other areas of your life—especially when you need something to think positive about. You can remember when you started something and it did not seem physically possible. I mean, something that seemed as though there was no way, but you do it and then you move on to the next goal that doesn't seem possible—only now you know that it is because you just did the last one. So, you know, it just gives you a good outlook in general. It keeps you positive and always gives you something to work toward.

Does climbing scare you?
YES.

So why do you continue to climb, and how do you deal with your fear?
Well, that's kind of my problem right now. Because I'm afraid to fall even though I know intellectually that it's safe, I feel like it's holding me back and I'm not progressing at the rate at which I should. So I am trying to get over that concern. To help get over that fear, I am surrounding myself with positive people whom I can trust to catch me when I fall off. I've also been trying to just push myself. For example, if I go back to a route that I've done before but fell off, that is frustrating and gets me a little fired up. I know I can do the route because I've done it before, so then I'll try harder and focus less on the fear and more on the fact that I know I can do it.

Do you think that climbing has impacted other areas of your life? If so, what and how?
Well, especially since I work a "regular" job with "regular" hours, I tend to associate with people in similar situations and lifestyles. Climbing, however, has introduced me to different types of people, adventures, viewpoints, and attitudes, and I think that's been really exciting.

Marie-Andree Cloutier climbing *Pure Palm* (5.11a) in the Lower Gorge at Smith Rock, Oregon.

My motto has always been that the best training for climbing is to climb. There are so many new skills, techniques, and other "tricks" to climbing, and the more you climb, the more you and your body will figure out all of these things. Your pool of techniques from which to draw upon will become deeper. This, for the beginner, is going to be the best training.

Furthermore, climbing relies heavily on tendon strength, particularly in your fingers, hands, forearms, and elbows. Problem is, your muscles develop faster than your tendons. So while you may feel strong and ready to start a strict training regimen, this could quite possibly put you at a high risk for tendon injury.

If you feel, however, that you have been climbing for a while and want to step it up, you can start with some basic training.

> My motto has always been that the best training for climbing is climbing.

Basic Training Schedule

To start simple, it's best to climb three or four days a week. Climbing is largely anaerobic (as opposed to aerobic, such as running), so you won't improve if you're climbing every day. Getting on a schedule of climbing and resting days will be your first step toward training. Many people find the following schedule works best for them:

Monday: Rest
Tuesday: Climb
Wednesday: Rest
Thursday: Climb
Friday: Rest
Saturday: Climb
Sunday: Rest or climb, depending on energy level

Advanced Body Positions

Once you've gotten the hang of the basic body positions that we discussed in chapter 3, you can start trying some advanced body positions.

Katie Brown on *Joe Six Pack* (5.13a), Virgin River Gorge, Arizona.

Heel Hooking

Heel hooking is a great way of taking weight off your arms, particularly on steep walls. It also helps to keep your hips tucked into the wall and can enable you to use your legs to maximum efficiency. Heel hooking is basically what it sounds like, but there are ways to make it work better. First, it's going to work best on holds that have a lip or edge on them, since the rubber on your shoe is going to stick better that way. Furthermore, don't just plunk your foot down on the hold. You want to turn your hip and foot out and point your toe, getting your pelvis as close to the wall as possible. When you pull with your heel to reach the next hold, you should feel the pull in your hamstring.

Toe Hooking

Similar to heel hooking, toe hooking is just what it sounds like. In fact, the whole concept is very similar. The only difference is that you toe hook when a hold is facing in the opposite direction of a hold that is suitable for heel hooking. Toe hooking is very good when climbing a horizontal roof, for example. Hook your toe around a hold and pull. You should feel it in the front of your shin, and in a roof it can help you relax your core for a moment.

A heel hook allows you to pull up in conjunction with your upper body muscles. It is very useful when pulling over roofs or on steep walls where there are few if any holds to stand on. A heel hook is also an effective way to rest. The pulling action of your leg can take quite a bit of weight off your arms.

A toe hook is very useful, particularly on steep rock. It can help you rest, help take weight off your upper body, help you utilize a foothold you couldn't otherwise use, and help control potential swings.

Flagging

Flagging is a way of balancing your body when it's in a position where it's unbalanced or you only have one foothold. Think of your leg acting as a rudder, guiding your body in the correct direction. For many, flagging is a hard concept to understand, but once you get it, it will do wonders for your climbing.

Left: When you "flag" your leg it acts as a ballast to keep your body balanced. Flagging can also generate power and help guide your body in the intended direction.
Above: You can also flag your leg on the inside of your body to help stabilize your stance.

Knee Bars and Knee Scums

Knee bars are a great way to take the weight off your arms when, for example, your handholds are very bad. A knee bar can also help you rest. To knee bar, you're going to brace your leg from foot to knee between two holds. Sometimes you can't get a full knee bar, so you have to settle for a knee scum. This will take a bit more energy and tension from your leg but will still help take weight off your arms. Many people will glue a piece of sticky rubber to a knee pad and slide it onto their thigh to help the knee bar stay in place better.

Sometimes a good knee bar is just the ticket.

Penduluming

Penduluming is the idea of taking a hold in the direction that it wants to be taken. Don't keep your body very stiff or rigid. Sometimes a hold will be facing in a direction that will dictate which way your body moves. Allow your body to pivot under the hold rather than staying in the four-point position.

Dynamic Movements

There are several different kinds of dynamic movements, going from a quick, upward hand movement to all-out four-points-off dyno.

Deadpointing

Deadpointing is basically a quick hand movement. Your body is fairly stable, but your hand movement is dynamic, requiring precision and good contact strength. You'll often need to deadpoint if, for example, one handhold is quite bad but you have to move off it. Letting go with one hand will be hard, so you'll be required to move very quickly to catch the next hold before falling off the bad one.

Lunging

Lunging involves more of the whole body, when you're not necessarily losing contact with the rock, but are making a large, dynamic movement from hold to hold. To lunge, you're going to start with your feet and push with your legs, hips, abs, and arms in one fluid, upward movement. Lunging generates a lot of power and allows you to maximize your strength when needing to move quickly.

1. When lunging, first focus on the hold you are lunging to.

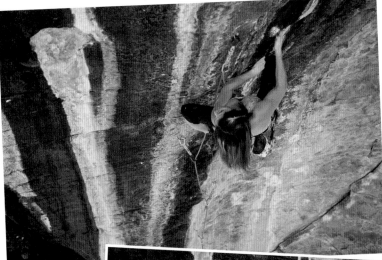

2. Compress your body, then push with your feet in a springing motion.

3. Aim for the hold. Believe you can grab it.

4. When your fingers make contact, hang on for all you're worth.

The dyno

A dyno is when your feet—and on rare occasions, your arms as well—lose contact with the rock and you are literally jumping from one hold to the other. This is done in the same way as a lunge, the difference being that you are going to push off your footholds and jump to the next hold. This is needed when, for example, your foothold is too far below you to reach the next hand-hold and there are no intermediate feet to use.

3. Release all points of contact with the wall and go for that hold!

2. Spring upward using your legs and arms—but mostly your legs.

1. When dynoing, first crouch to compress your body.

Other Training Tactics

Below are some additional techniques to use as you push your climbing ability to the next level.

"Working" a Route

Try picking a route that is too hard for you—this means a route that you cannot climb successfully on your first try without falling or resting—and practice it until you can successfully climb it from bottom to top. This is called "working" a route, and once you are successful on it, it's called "redpointing." While working routes is a very good way to increase strength and perfect specific skills, it is also a great tool for training. Picking a route to redpoint will give you a goal to focus on, and once you've succeeded, it can give you an immense feeling of satisfaction that you might be lacking if you are just going to the gym two nights a week for an hour.

On-sighting

Pick a route at a grade that is difficult for you, and try to climb it your first try without falling. This is called "on-sighting." Tell yourself before you begin climbing that you are not going to hang and rest—you are going to climb until you fall, ideally reaching the top of the climb before that happens. On-sighting will immensely help your endurance, as you will have to conserve your energy, rest when the opportunity arises, climb through a pump, and pause while figuring out the best way to climb the section above you.

Flashing

Flashing a route is when you either watch someone climb a route or have someone tell you the best way to climb it, and then climb said route on your first try without falling. Practicing flashing is going to help you learn how to "read" a route. You see, climbing isn't as simple as just grabbing holds and moving upward. Once you start improving your skills, you will notice that there are multiple ways to do a single move, from the most energy-efficient way to the least. That being said, reading a route is the ability to tell from the ground the best and most efficient way to climb it. Either watching other climbers before you or having someone more experienced give you "beta" (specific information about how to do moves) is going to help teach you how to read routes.

Developing a Climbing Strategy

Once you have spent some time climbing, you will begin to learn what grades are consistently easy for you, moderately difficult, very difficult, etc. The best way to maximize your climbing day—and perhaps one of the most fundamental stepping stones toward developing a training routine—is to have a bit of strategy in your climbing. This includes a proper warm-up, workout, and cool-down.

The Warm-Up

Begin on routes that are very easy for you. Trying a route too hard too soon will result in a "flash pump." This is when you get very pumped very quickly because your muscles aren't warmed up. Not properly warming up can also cut your climbing day short because you will feel exhausted far more quickly. Also, if you try something too hard too soon, this will unduly fatigue you for the rest of the day. Generally speaking, three or four routes are good for warming up, starting with a very easy one and progressing to a route that will get you somewhat pumped but that you won't fall off of.

The Workout

To maximize your climbing day, you don't want to just climb willy-nilly. Once you're warmed up, get on your "project," or a route that is very hard for you and you cannot do from bottom to top without falling. Work out the moves, then try to redpoint the route once or twice, depending on your energy level. If you're successful, great—this means next time you need to try something a bit harder. If not, don't worry about it—you can try it again next time. From here, you're going to take a step down to something slightly less hard that you may have redpointed before. Again, do one or two routes at this level. If you're still feeling energetic, take another step down and do two to four routes that are hard for you but that you usually don't fall on. This general principle can also be applied to bouldering.

The Cool-Down

Often overlooked, cooling down is important to help work out the lactic acid in your system so that you're less sore the next day. Climb a couple of easy routes to cool down, followed by a bit of stretching.

Setting Goals

Setting goals for yourself is a great and very simple way to encourage your climbing to the next level. Say there's a move on a particular route that you can never quite get. Rather than giving up, decide that you are going to practice other moves that are similar and that within a month of practice you are going to stick that move. Or decide that you are going to work your way up to being able to climb eight different routes within a climbing day. Giving your climbing day a bit of focus or intent can help immensely.

Mental Training

Sometimes the hardest part of climbing is the mental aspect. Climbing is very mentally challenging on a lot of different levels, particularly for women, so it's important to start mental training early on. One of the main mental struggles within climbing is fear, which I've addressed in previous chapters. Following are some other mental challenges within climbing.

Katie Brown on *Dead Man Walking* (5.9+), a limestone trad climb at El Potrero Chico, Mexico.

Focus

It's easy to get distracted while climbing, and when you're distracted, it's hard to concentrate on the task at hand. Problem is, climbing requires a good deal of concentration. It's not a sport where you can let your mind wander. You must constantly assess your situation, figuring out where to put your foot, where to put your hand, how to shift your body to best reach the next hold, etc.

Practice climbing when there is a lot going on around you, such as during a busy evening in the gym or when your girlfriends are down at the base of a route gossiping about something that you desperately want to hear. There's no better training for focus than to practice focusing. Concentrate on each move individually, listening to your body move. Tune out everything going on around and below you. If you are familiar with the route you are about to climb, close your eyes and visualize each move before you begin, like a mantra, until there is no room in your head for anything but the moves you are about to execute. The ability to focus will also play a part in some of the other mental games we play with ourselves, as discussed below.

Expectations

Another pitfall within your mental climbing "game" is expectations. It's easy to place undue expectations upon yourself or to assume that others around you are expecting things of you. Either way, it is a heavy burden to bear, and it can take all the luster out of your climbing. To counter this, practice being reasonable with your expectations. Recognize that you can't control the variables around you—you can only control how hard you try in that particular situation. You can no more control the weather than you can control what others may or may not expect of you, so therefore these things don't matter, right? They don't, but at the same time, they may be present, so recognize uncontrollable factors around you and then put them aside, focusing instead on your individual effort.

Fatigue

When you get tired on a climb, it's easy to panic and begin to think negatively about the potential outcome of your effort. When you're on a climb and you feel your mind begin to shift from the task at hand to how tired you are, make a conscious effort to shift it back to your climb. Think about what's ahead of you rather than the possibility of falling. As I've mentioned before, break the climb down to one move at a time. As you focus on each move ahead of you, you may suddenly find yourself clipping the anchor in spite of your fatigue.

Confidence

How confident we are in our strength and skills as a climber can greatly affect our performance on the rock. If you are about to try a route that you know is going to be very hard for you, it's easy to let negative thoughts about how you will perform crowd your mind. Practice positive thinking and self-affirmations before beginning, telling yourself that you are strong and that you can do this route. Leave no room in your mind for negativity, and don't leave the ground until each negative thought has been countered by a positive one.

Additionally, it's easy to lose confidence while climbing. Say you fumble on a move that you've done a hundred times before and suddenly you're thinking, "What is happening? I must be having a bad day! Oh my, I'm so tired, and the crux is coming up!" This is not a good mind frame to be in. Again, tell yourself that it doesn't matter and keep moving ahead, focusing on what's coming rather than the move you just messed up. Or, say you're trying to on-sight a route and you reach a section where you're not sure how to get past it. Rather than focusing on the possibility that you may choose the wrong way and fall, concentrate on listening to your instincts. Instincts can go a long way. What are they telling you? Then, once you commit, commit all the way, even if it doesn't feel perfect right away. Don't quit until you fall. Let your body do the work rather than your brain—you may surprise yourself.

Non-Climbing Training

Core Strength

Core strength plays a large part in climbing. If your core is strong, you are going to have an immense advantage. You're going to be better able to maintain a position, hold your body taut, and make the best use of your limbs. Doing some core-strengthening exercises as part of your cool-down can be a great start to implementing a training program.

Flexibility

Flexibility, like core strength, can greatly benefit your climbing. Again, it's a great idea to incorporate stretching into your cool-down routine.

Strength Conditioning

Climbing works a wide variety of muscles, but at the same time, there are certain muscle groups that get overlooked. Strength training your antagonistic muscles so that they do not atrophy can not only go a long way toward avoiding injury, but can also help balance out your strength and help your overall climbing performance.

Don't leave the ground until each negative thought has been countered by a positive one.

story

A Lesson in Redpointing

Before this book went into production, I was asked to add a few personal narrative sidebars. Several topics were suggested by the editor, including:

1. Route you've worked the hardest on and succeeded
2. Route you've worked the hardest on and not succeeded

At the time I thought, "Well, I know the perfect route for the second one." You see, I've never been very good at redpointing. It's the aspect of climbing that I've struggled with since the beginning, and I've always envied those who are good at it. For many, many years I would get on routes, and if I couldn't do it in three or four tries—tops—I would give up.

The thing is, redpointing routes is hard. It's an entirely different skill than on-sighting, with its own unique set of challenges. Some people consider redpointing easier because you get to practice the moves and become familiar and confident with the route. You're able to discover the most efficient way to do each move, whereas when on-sighting, every move and moment is a surprise and you must be constantly adapting to each situation that arises.

But for me, redpointing is pretty much the most frustrating thing ever. The more I get on a route, the more I become aware of exactly where I'm going to be scared, where it's going to be hard, and where I'll probably fall. This, then, only makes me dread getting on the route, and sometimes it seems that the more I try a route, the more I start hating it.

But I digress . . . Three winters ago, I came upon a route called *Playing Hooky* on a feature known as the Tombstone, about five minutes outside of Moab, Utah, where I live. It's a four-pitch route, and the grades are 5.10, 5.12-, 5.13-, and 5.12-. The moment I saw it, I decided that it was the route for me. I loved it, everything about it, and I strung up a rope and proceeded to work on it. I would go out early in the morning and climb on the route, relishing the quiet alone time, the aesthetic nature of the route, the moment when the sun hit the wall, warming me and the rock around me. I thoroughly enjoyed my time on the Tombstone, but then I started thinking about trying to redpoint it—and I started to get nervous.

I tried leading the third pitch—the crux—and I got scared. I tried again, and I got scared again. I did this for a week or so, and I got not only increasingly frustrated with the route, but even more so, increasingly frustrated with myself and my inability to redpoint. So I gave up and walked away.

All summer I climbed elsewhere and enjoyed myself, but the Tombstone stayed in the back of my head. By September I felt brave enough to try again, so I found a partner and up we went, setting out at 5:00 a.m. to avoid the heat that still lingered in Moab that time of year. I worked every move out perfectly on toprope, then worked my gear out, then committed to leading the pitch. I actually gave it a solid effort that time around, taking falls and trying hard. Still, even though I could climb the pitch easily on toprope, I would literally scare myself off on each redpoint burn. After four or five tries, and four or five falls, my partner left town and the Tombstone once again fell by the wayside. I decided to just give up forever, like I had on every other route that I'd failed repeatedly on.

I just wasn't a redpoint climber, I told myself—and that was okay. A part of me felt that if I could just get over that hump and redpoint something, then maybe it would open the door to being able to redpoint other things as well. But I just couldn't seem to get over that hump. I didn't want to deal with the repeated failure and frustration. It was just easier to stick to what I was good at.

All that winter and the next summer I climbed. I even on-sighted a 5.13 crack, and got somewhat back into sport-climbing shape. I told myself I was never going to get on the Tombstone again—but it still nagged at me every time I drove by it to go for a run or a hike.

That's where I thought the story would end—the route that I worked on the hardest and failed. But then winter came to Moab again, and it was particularly cold and snowy. If I wanted to climb, I was limited to the very warmest of walls. I ended up on a route called *Pink Flamingo,* a 5.13 crack that was the worst size imaginable for my little hands. It was also a route that I had tried a couple times before and then declared too hard. Here I was, though, with not a lot of options. I started working on it, and many tries later, managed to redpoint it. As I clipped the chains I realized that I had actually succeeded on a route that had not come easily to me. I had stuck with it in spite of the perceived failure and consequent frustration. I was over the hump.

A huge smile formed on my face and the image of the Tombstone floated into my brain. Maybe, just maybe, I should give it another try. It was the perfect time of year, I was in great crack-climbing shape, and I was officially over the redpointing hump. Of course, I had forgotten all of the sequences and gear placements that I had worked out the year before, so I figured I was starting over at square one. Once again, I strung up a toprope and prepared myself for the process of working the route.

My friend Cory went up the route with

me that day. Before I started the crux pitch, I said to him, "Okay, just keep the rope kinda tight here, because this first little boulder problem is really hard for me." I started climbing and noticed immediately that each finger lock seemed somehow so much better than I remembered. Every move seemed considerably easier, and I climbed right through the boulder problem.

"Weird!" I yelled down to Cory. "That was so easy. I thought for sure I was going to have to figure out the beta just perfectly!" I continued climbing, and before I knew it, I was at the anchor. I was so excited, I was jumping out of my shoes. The route felt so easy! I lowered down and climbed the pitch twice more. "Well," I said, "I guess I'm ready to lead the route. That was strange how easy it felt."

I rested the following day and worried that it was some kind of weird fluke that the route had felt so easy. I didn't sleep that night, and the next day had knots in my stomach as I racked up to start the climb. I wanted to do this climb SO bad, and I wasn't even sure why. My teeth chatter when I'm nervous, and they were yammering away. My climbing partner looked at me strangely.

"Are you really cold or something?"

"No," I said. "Just nervous."

"Okay. You're a strange one."

"Mm-hmm," I muttered, too distracted to notice his comment. "Okay, here we go."

And I was off: first pitch, second pitch, then the crux pitch. My teeth clattered in my head, and I clenched my jaw shut to stop it. I procrastinated at the anchor for as long

as possible, but eventually I had nothing left to do. I had to start climbing.

I unclipped from the anchor and started on my way, making it through the boulder problem pretty well. Up I went, placing the impossibly thin gear as I climbed. I tried to breathe deeply and stay calm, but I could feel myself shaking with fear, nervousness, and the pure, unadulterated desire to climb this pitch without falling. At one point my foot slipped off and I gasped.

"Crap," I thought to myself. "Stay calm and do not fall. You are not going to fall. Don't you dare fall."

I stuffed in more gear than necessary and continued climbing, feeling my rib cage compress in relief as I grabbed the final hold past the crux and breathed out in disbelief. Panting and pumped, I made my way up through the final wide, layback section of the pitch and clipped the anchor.

"Oh my god, I did it! I redpointed something!" I was so excited, I could hardly believe it. I felt a little stupid about being so excited, but I couldn't help it—I was excited. And relieved, so incredibly relieved. A huge wave of relaxation rushed through my body, and I had to remind myself that I still had one more pitch left.

I hadn't been on the last pitch since the very first time I had been up the Tombstone, and I remembered it being bad rock, scary, and surprisingly hard. Somehow, hanging at the anchor, I couldn't make myself care too much. I just kept hoping that it too would feel easier this time around.

As the sun dropped in the sky and the

The reward for redpointing a route includes relaxing at the belay with a great feeling of accomplishment.

temperature dipped, I started up the final pitch. The rock was nothing like comforting, and I passed a huge, chossy runout where there was no gear to be found. "Gawd," I thought to myself after finally clipping a decent piece of gear. "I hope I don't fall, because I do not want to do that section again."

At that point the rock angled back and opened into a dihedral with shallow, sandy pin scars for finger locks along the way. My feet stemmed on the blank, sand-encrusted wall on either side, and each move was a desperate attempt to combat the sand that separated my hands and the rubber on my shoes from the rock itself. I could feel, though, the determination in my body and

mind as I climbed, and I wasn't even scared anymore, even though the rock quality was terrible and my gear wasn't great. I was not going to give up.

Eventually I grabbed the final, sandy jug and pulled myself up over the lip and onto the top of the climb. There I stood on top of the Tombstone, that route that for whatever reason had thwarted me for so long. The sun turned the rock around me a bright orange as I belayed my partner up, and I marveled over this newfound ability to stick with routes. I can only hope that it carries over into other areas of my life, but even if it's strictly limited to climbing, I'm okay with that. I have finally learned how to redpoint.

Marieta Akalski boarding the
Mothership Connection, (5.13a),
El Potrero Chico, Mexico.

So, you've been climbing for some time now, and you have reached a bit of a plateau in terms of progressing to harder routes. This is to be expected. When you first begin climbing, 70 percent of what you need to improve upon falls within the categories of mental training and technique, while only 30 percent of your training needs to be devoted to sport-specific issues. As you improve, however, that ratio gradually changes to lean in the opposite direction. This may be the point that you are at. Your muscles, tendons, mind, and technique are all relatively solid, but you're not sure what exactly sport-specific training for climbing is. Well, that is where this chapter comes into play.

Advanced Training Basics

There are no set rules for how to train for climbing. There are, of course, books upon books on the subject, but it is my opinion that when it comes to climbing, every training program should be designed for the individual's needs, strengths, and weaknesses. At the same time, however, there are certain surefire methods and tools to make your training not only as effective as possible, but fun as well.

Determine Your Weaknesses

What is it that you need to work on? For me, it is always power. Endurance comes very easily to me, but power is a constant struggle. Also, I am much stronger on crimps than on slopers, or open-handed holds. Consequently, it is important for me to work on power and open-handed holds. It's easier,

Abbie Moore climbing *Tomcat* (5.10+), Indian Creek, Utah.

however, for me to gravitate toward those things that cater to my strengths. I'm good at those things, so I have more fun doing them. If I put in the effort to work on my weaknesses, though, I find I enjoy climbing that much more because I feel stronger all around.

Mix It Up

It's important not to stagnate in your workouts. Doing the exact same workout every day isn't going to work either physically or mentally. Mixing up your workout will not only help keep you motivated, but will also confuse your body, thereby increasing your gains in overall performance over the long run.

Peaking

For many athletes, the idea behind training is to work toward a specific goal, such as a competition. This is called "peaking." If you are involved in an organized training program to run a marathon, for example, you will notice that your workouts gradually increase in intensity to a peak and then lessen, letting your body rest before the marathon. This will put your body in the best, but also most rested, position to perform at its optimal level.

While there is often no specific event to work toward in climbing, creating a goal can significantly help your motivation and overall performance. For example, say there is a route that you have always wanted to try but is at the outer limits of your skill and strength level. Your goal, then, is to try to on-sight it (climb it successfully without falling on your first try, with no previous knowledge of the route).

Following is a basic schedule to help you peak before your proposed goal.

Four Weeks of Skill and Stamina

For four weeks you are going to build a solid foundation of endurance and overall fitness. Your goal for these weeks is to log a lot of mileage. To gain endurance, you need to be doing a great many more moves than a handful, so if you're climbing on a route that is so hard for you that you're falling every several moves, this is going to be counterproductive. Pick routes that favor a variety of skills, but make sure they are one to three grades below your maximum ability level. You should be climbing up to four days a week, unless you are climbing to complete failure or at your maximum ability level.

Through this you should be (1) improv-ing your technique and overall climbing tactics and (2) improving general fitness and climbing-specific endurance.

Three Weeks of Power

For the next three weeks you are going to be focusing solely on power by bouldering, campus training, and other power exercises. Power training is very anaerobic, which means that you need a great deal of rest to recover from these types of workouts. It may seem as though you are not climbing very much during this phase, particularly in contrast to the past four weeks, but trust me, if you are truly bouldering at your maximum and campus training, you are going to need all the rest you can get. It's important to rest at least one day between climbs, and many people choose to climb on the schedule of one day on, two days off. If you feel energetic enough, however, it is fine to follow a one-day-on, one-day-off schedule.

Two Weeks of Power Endurance

Power endurance is somewhat of a no man's land within climbing. Essentially, it's more than five moves but less than thirty or forty. Power-endurance routes require a significant amount of power, in addition to enough endurance to continue at that high power level for an extended length of time. For two weeks you are going to focus on this area. Interval training (which I explain later in this chapter) is a great way to work on power endurance. You can also train this by climbing relatively short, high-intensity routes (or longish boulder problems) with a timed minimal amount of rest between burns. For example, try climbing as many routes as possible that are just below your maximum skill level within a ninety-minute time frame. You are going to be climbing one day on, two days off, no questions asked, so be sure to make the most of the training sessions that you do have!

Rest

Lastly, you are going to rest for a week. Don't be surprised if, on your first day back after this extended rest, you feel a bit stiff and even weak. This is a trick on your body. You are now in prime physical condition, but as a result of that fact and the amount of rest you've just gotten, it may take longer to warm up than you think it should.

Advanced Training Exercises

Now that you know the basic program of peaking, I'm going to tell you about some more specific training ideas that you can use to fulfill this program. You can employ these ideas at any time. Many of them are actually both a great workout and quite fun!

Exercises for Skill and Stamina
Blindfolding

Try strapping on a blindfold and climbing without sight. This exercise is good for training both technique and endurance. For starters, it takes you longer to get up the route without sight than with it. Also, and more importantly, you are forced to rely on your remaining senses to get you up the route. This means that you are truly going to have to listen to your body and your instincts. Often, you'll find out after the fact that, for example, you may have stood on a far smaller hold than you would have trusted, should you have been able to actually see its size.

"Beep"

This game is one of my favorites, but it only works if you are climbing with a fairly sizable group of people. One person acts as route setter and everyone else must go somewhere out of sight. The route setter creates a long boulder problem (twenty to thirty moves), then calls everyone back into the room and points out the holds on the route one time and one time only. Everyone goes back to where they cannot watch the other climbers, then each person comes out one at a time and tries out their memory. If a wrong hold is grabbed, the route setter says "beep" and the climber must go back one move, and then continue on. If a wrong hold is grabbed a second time, the climber must go back two moves in the problem, and so on. Once the climber's turn is complete (having either fallen off or successfully climbed the route), he or she can watch all subsequent climbers. You can then take turns being the route setter to get in a great, fun endurance workout.

Five minutes on, two minutes off

The goal here is to stay on the wall for five minutes. If you're bouldering, just don't touch the ground. If you're on a route, you can downclimb and then start up another route. Time yourself, and once the timer goes off, set it again for two minutes—this is your rest time. Repeat this cycle five times. Or, if you don't feel like being quite so precise, you can do this with a partner. Climb two or three routes (depending on how long they are) in a row, and then switch with your partner. The key to this is that you make sure you are climbing one after another and not getting any additional rest.

Exercises for Power
Bouldering
A very simple way of training for power is just by having a bouldering session with several friends. Take turns making up hard, short (less than ten moves) boulder problems and trying them. If you're making up your own boulder problems, it's good to climb with other people because everyone's style is different and you will probably end up testing each other's weaknesses.

Theme boulder problems
Create a series of boulder problems that focus on a single theme: a sloper problem, a crimper problem, a problem with big moves, etc.

Campus Board Exercises
There is a never-ending number of things you can do on a campus board, but here I'm just going to give you a few to get you started. Any of these exercises can be done with or without your feet, depending on your strength level.

Contact strength
Most campus boards are numbered. If the one you're working with isn't, then just count them out. Start with both hands on the bottom rung (rung 1). Pop one hand up to rung 3, pausing just long enough to make sure you've got the hold solidly, then bump that hand back down to rung 1. Repeat with your other hand without resting, and repeat this cycle five times with each hand.

Lock-off
Start with both hands on rung 1. With your left hand, lock off the bottom rung and reach as high as you can with your right hand. You don't have to hit a rung, because it is your bottom hand that you're training. Hold the position for three to five seconds, then lower both hands back to the bottom rung. Repeat with your other hand; again, do this five times with each hand.

Traditional campusing
Start with both hands on rung 1 and bump one hand to rung 3. Without matching your other hand on rung 3, go to rung 5 with the opposite hand. Continue on up the campus board in this manner if you can. If you can't, drop off and repeat, reversing your hand sequence. Yet again, do this five times on each hand.

Lisa Hensel climbing *Tom Cat*, a 5.10+ crack corner at Indian Creek, Utah.

Dynamic campusing

On the largest campus rungs available, try to jump both your hands at the same time to the next rung. Bump your hands back down again, and do this five times.

Exercises for Power Endurance
4x4s

Once you're warmed up, begin doing sets of four boulder problems. Pick two that are quite hard for you and two that are moderately hard. Climb the harder two first, then the easier two, all in a row. This should be quite hard, but try your best to climb all four without falling. Rest for fifteen minutes and repeat the process until you are consistently falling on the problems (three to five repetitions).

Interval training

The 4x4s are a type of interval training, and this exercise is very similar, only done with routes instead of boulder problems. You're going to be doing sets of four routes consecutively—a hard one, an easy one, a hard one, an easy one. Rest for fifteen to twenty minutes between sets, and do this three to five times.

Climb until you fall

Pick a route that you can do all the moves on, but which you sometimes fall on. Climb until you fall, then get immediately back on and continue. Lower to the ground and start again. Repeat this three to five times.

The Importance of Rest

Rest is something that is often overlooked, but it is of the utmost importance to a training program. In some ways, rest is actually more important than the actual training.

After a period of rigorous training, your body is temporarily weakened. It then reacts to this weakened state by preparing itself to do its designated task better the next time. This adaptive reaction to training is called "supercompensation." The trick, though, is learning how much rest the body needs to reach supercompensation. If you climb again before you have fully recovered, you will not be able to acquire all the benefits of your earlier training session. Repeating this mistake will then actually result in a loss of performance ability. If you climb again at the exact point of recovery from the last training session, your performance will plateau. It is only when you go past that exact point of recovery and reach supercompensation that you will see improvements.

So how much rest is enough? That depends on the type and amount of training being done. Obviously, there is no strict, cut-and-dry answer. As a point of reference, however, experts recommend anywhere from twenty-four to seventy-two hours. In his book *Training for Climbing,* Eric J. Hörst gives an example: "[I]t might take only one day to recover from a high volume of low-intensity activity like climbing a bunch of really easy routes, whereas it would probably take three or more days to recover completely from a high volume of high-intensity exercise, such as climbing a bunch of routes near your limit."

Hörst then goes on to list the three major recovery periods that the body goes through on its road to supercompensation. The first recovery period extends from ten seconds to thirty minutes after a workout. This would be, for example, the amount of time that you typically spend resting between routes during a day of cragging. Next is the refuel recovery period—thirty minutes to twenty-four hours after exercise. The majority of your refueling during this period will take place in about sixteen hours. This means, then, that the average twelve-hour break between consecutive climbing days will allow your body to recover to only about 80 percent of its capacity.

It is during the third recovery period, therefore, that gains in ability are actually being made. If you have ever been sorer on your second day of rest than on your first, you know what I am talking about. This is called "delayed onset muscle soreness," or DOMS. During strenuous exercise your muscle fibers are damaged microscopically. The amount of DOMS that you feel, then, will be equal to the amount of damage that your muscles have experienced. If the DOMS is only minor, it can fade within forty-eight hours. If you have much greater soreness, however, it is possible that it will take four or more days for your muscle fibers to repair themselves.

While all this information is great, resting still comes down to a feeling. It is essen-

If I put in the effort to work on my weaknesses, though, I find I enjoy climbing that much more because I feel stronger all around.

tial for a climber to learn how to listen to her body. Learn to pay attention and to listen to what your body is telling you. Like all other animals, we have instincts and our bodies know instinctively what we need— so long as we don't let our minds get in the way. The body knows better, and is more reliable, than any advice from a book, person, or the Internet.

Perhaps the best way to assess the state of your body was told to me by a friend who is a former professional cyclist. "You should

always feel one step behind," he said. In saying this, he meant that you should always be eager and energetic for the next workout. If you're dragging your feet, feeling lackluster, and finding that your performance is suffering, perhaps this is your body's way of telling you that you aren't allowing yourself adequate rest.

In addition, occasionally take extended periods of rest. Throughout the year, break up your training for climbing with stretches of activity that promote recovery (for example, running, skipping rope, swimming, or biking). Don't be afraid to take at least a week off, and to do this several times a year.

> Don't be afraid to take at least a week off, and to do this several times a year.

Brittany Griffith on the *East Face* of Monkey Face (5.12c), Smith Rock, Oregon.

interview

Brittany Griffith climbing *Sentry Box* (5.12a) in Squamish, British Columbia.

Professional climber **Brittany Griffith** has been climbing for over ten years. Here, she tells us a bit about what climbing means to her and also lists—in her usual sarcastic way—her top ten tips for success on the rocks:

I started climbing relatively late in life—twenty-five. I was a girl from Iowa and a boyfriend asked me if I wanted to go on a road trip.

"What's a road trip?" I naively asked. He explained that it was when you traveled around rock climbing and mountain biking. I had a mountain bike but didn't know the first thing about climbing. I faked my way through this minor detail and agreed.

Confession: The very first day I ever tried climbing was the first day of this road trip (Vedavoo, Wyoming). My attraction to the sport was immediate. The lifestyle really appealed to me—living, eating, waking, sleeping, and playing outdoors. I had never felt so natural in my whole life. It was the first thing that ever really made sense to me. I loved the adventure and the mental and physical challenges climbing presented. It was a great game.

I am not especially talented, nor driven enough, to be an amazing climber, so I never wholeheartedly tried. The only undeniable aspect I possess, since that day in May almost thirteen years ago, is that I truly love it. All of it: the success, failure, frustration, elation, fear, confidence, anxiety, and peace. My life revolves around climbing, yet somehow I feel I am not defined by it. My happiness is not dependent on how hard I climb, only that I do it. My friends do not have to be climbers, but they somehow all are. I spend little time talking or thinking about climbing, but it is omnipresent nonetheless. Yet, I repeatedly argue that climbing is mere exercise. This, however, is a veil. I guess the real trick to success in something is diminishing its importance to you.

Oh, yeah, I was supposed to give you my top ten tips for success on the rocks. Fine. Here they are:

10. Commit at least fifteen hours a week to climbing.
9. Maintain general physical fitness (a small beer belly is okay).
8. Identify a weakness each time you climb.
7. Consider doing something about this weakness.
6. Check your knot.
5. Clean your shoes.
4. Always thank your belayer.
3. Always cheer for your partner, even on the warm-ups.
2. Try to control your emotions or they will control you.
1. Use your feet.

Katie Brown climbing the beautiful *Tombstone Crack* (5.10d), on the Monument at Smith Rock, Oregon.

My question at this point is: After all that training, are you still enjoying yourself, or do you feel weighed down by training regimes, the need to improve, or numbers and goals? Can you still remember why you initially started climbing and why you picked up this book? Was it for the adventure, to be empowered to try a new sport, to conquer a fear, to share a sport with your children, or to enjoy the movement and strength of your body? Whatever the reason, I want to remind you here to never forget that feeling.

As you know, I started climbing when I was thirteen. By the time I was twenty, I hated climbing and everything it had become. I trained and trained, and pushed myself and pushed myself, to the point that I simply did it because it was all I knew and it was what I did, and I would force myself through each day of climbing. It got to the point where I couldn't remember anymore what it was I had loved about climbing in the first place. And why? Because I got burned out but didn't give myself a break. I kept training anyway. Rock climbing was my whole life and I became very one-dimensional—and I am not a one-dimensional person. I wanted to write a book; I wanted to learn to dance, to go to school, to have friends, to go out at night, to sing at open-mike night sometime. In the end, I completely quit climbing for nearly two years, before I finally achieved enough distance from the sport to remember why I loved it.

While this is an extreme case, what I'm trying to share with you is that it's so important to keep things in perspective, to make sure that you are still participating in the sport for the "right" reasons. Climbing is so magical, but it's so easy to lose that and get caught up in the numbers game or the pursuit to get better. Don't be afraid, within your climbing, to stop and smell the roses, so to speak.

Some things to remember:

- Embrace your fears.

- Trust your instincts.

- Move your body—it's a vertical dance.

- Climb because you love it.

- Holding on to a rock can actually free your mind, body, and soul.

- Above all, feel the magic and enjoy!

appendix a:
rock climbing glossary

aid: Means of getting up a climb using other than the actions of hands, feet, and body English.

aid climb: To climb using equipment for direct assistance, which allows passage over rock otherwise impossible using only hands and feet; opposite of *free climb*.

Aliens: A type of spring-loaded camming devices (SLCDs), the most popular types of anchors. See **Friends.**

anchor: A means by which climbers are secured to a cliff.

anchor matrix: The placement of anchors using various rigging systems.

arête: An outside edge or corner of rock, like the outer spine of a book, sometimes as large as a mountain ridge.

arm bar: A means of holding on to a wide crack; also called *arm lock*.

arm lock: See arm bar.

backstep: The climbing move of placing the outside edge of the foot behind, usually on a vertical hold.

bashie: A piece of malleable metal that has been hammered into a rock seam as an anchor; used in extreme aid climbing.

belay: Procedure of securing a climber by the use of a rope.

Beta: Specific information provided by one climber to another about how to do the moves on a route or boulder problem.

bi-doigt: A two-finger handhold.

Big Dudes: A type of spring-loaded camming devices (SLCDs), the most popular types of anchors. See **Friends.**

big wall: See **wall.**

bight: A loop, as in a bight of rope.

biner: See **carabiner.**

bolt: An artificial anchor placed in a hole drilled for that purpose.

bomber: Absolutely fail-safe (as in a very solid anchor or big, big handhold); sometimes called *bombproof.*

bombproof: See **bomber.**

bridging: See **stemming.**

bucket: A handhold large enough to fully latch onto, like the handle of a bucket.

buttress: An outside edge of rock that's much broader than an arête, definitely mountain-size.

cam: To lodge in a crack by counterpressure; that which lodges.

Camalots: A type of spring-loaded camming devices (SLCDs), the most popular types of anchors. See **Friends.**

carabiner: Aluminum alloy ring equipped with a spring-loaded snap gate; sometimes called *biner* or *krab.*

ceiling: A section of rock that extends out above your head; an overhang of sufficient size to loom overhead; also called a *roof.*

chalk: Standard equipment used to soak up finger and hand sweat on holds, although not allowed at certain areas.

chickenhead: A bulbous knob of rock.

chimney: A crack of sufficient size to accept an entire body.

chock: See nut.

chockstone: A rock lodged in a crack.

Class 1: Mountain travel classification for trail hiking.

Class 2: Mountain travel classification for hiking over rough ground, such as scree and talus; may include the use of hands for stability.

Class 3: Mountain travel classification for scrambling that requires the use of hands and careful foot placement.

Lisa Hensel placing gear on an
Indian Creek, Utah, 5.12.

Class 4: Mountain travel classification for scrambling over steep and exposed terrain; a rope may be used for safety on exposed areas.

Class 5: Mountain travel classification for technical free climbing where terrain is steep and exposed, requiring the use of ropes, protection hardware, and related techniques.

Class 6: Mountain travel classification for aid climbing where climbing equipment is used for balance, rest, or progress, denoted with a capital letter A followed by numerals 0 to 5 (for example, 5.9/A3, meaning the free-climbing difficulties are up to 5.9 with an aid section of A3 difficulty). Also see **Yosemite Decimal System (YDS).**

clean: Routes that are variously free of vegetation or loose rock, or where you don't need to place pitons; also the act of removing chocks and other gear from a pitch.

cling grip: A handhold where you grasp an edge with your fingers.

cold shut: A relatively soft metal ring that can be closed with a hammer blow; notoriously unreliable for withstanding high loads; commonly found as anchors atop short sport climbs.

cordelette: Standard tackle that facilitates equalizing the load between two or more anchors. A sixteen-foot section of six-millimeter Spectra is tied into a loop and clipped through all the anchor pieces, then tied off to create a single tie-in point, forming separate and equalized loops.

crack: Type of irregularity on the stone.

crimper: A small but positive sharp edge.

crux: The most difficult section of a climb or pitch, typically marked on topos with the difficulty rating.

difficulty rating: See **Classes 1–6, Grades I–VI, R-rated, X-rated,** and **Yosemite Decimal System (YDS).**

dihedral: An inside corner of the climbing surface, formed by two planes of rock, like the oblique angle formed by the pages in an open book.

downclimb, downclimbing: A descent without rope, usually when rappelling is unsafe or impractical.

drag: Used in reference to the resistance of rope running through carabiners.

dynamic: Lunge move; sometimes called a *dynamo* or *mo.*

dynamo: See **dynamic.**

dyno: A move where all points of contact leave the wall as the climber jumps up to reach a hold that could not otherwise be reached.

edge: A small hold ledge or the act of standing on an edge.

edging: The climbing move of placing the very edge of the shoe on any hold that is clear-cut.

exposure: A relative situation where a climb has particularly noticeable sheerness.

flake: Type of irregularity on the stone.

flag: Using a limb as a counterbalance.

flash: Free climbing a route from bottom to top on first try.

footwork: The art and method of standing on holds.

free: See **free climb.**

free ascent: See **free climb.**

free climb: The upward progress gained by a climber's own efforts, using hands and feet on available features, unaided or free of attending ropes and gear. Rope is only used to safeguard against injury, not for upward progress or resting; opposite of *aid climb;* also called *free* or *free ascent.*

free solo: Free climbing a route alone from bottom to top on your first try.

Friends: Spring-loaded camming devices (SLCDs) that can be used in all situations; the most popular type of anchors. These include Aliens, Big Dudes, Camalots, Quad Cams, and Three-Cam Units (TCUs).

frog step: A climbing move where you bring one foot up, then the other, while keeping your torso at the same level, forming a crouched, or "bullfrog," position.

gobies: Hand abrasions.

grade: A rating that tells how much time an experienced climber will take on a given climb; the "overall seriousness" grade (referring to the level of commitment, overall technical difficulty, ease of escape, and length of route), denoted by Roman numerals.

Grade I: A climb that may take only a few hours to complete, such as Class 4 scrambles and Class 5 climbs.

Grade II: A climb that may take three to four hours.

Grade III: A climb that may take four to six hours, a strong half-day.

Grade IV: A climb that may take a full day.

Grade V: A climb that may take one or two days and involve technical difficulties, weather, and other objective hazards, such as rockfall or avalanche danger. A bivouac is usually unavoidable.

Grade VI: A climb that may take two or more days on the wall.

greasy: Used to describe a slick surface.

hangdog: When a leader hangs from a piece of protection to rest, then continues on without lowering down; not a *free ascent*.

headwall: A much steeper section of cliff, residing toward the top.

heel hooking: The attempt to use the foot as a hand, usually on a vertical climb, where the heel is kicked over the head and hooked over a large hold.

Hex: See **Hexentric.**

Hexentric: Brand name (made by Black Diamond) of a six-sided or barrel-shaped anchor that can be wedged into wide cracks and bottlenecks; sometimes called a *Hex.*

horn: A flake-like projection of rock, generally of small size.

jam: Wedging feet, hands, fingers, or other body parts to gain purchase in a crack.

jug: A big hold that can be grabbed easily, like a jug handle.

kneedrop: Climbing move where the knee is dropped low and the rump is right over the foot.

krab: See **carabiner.**

layback, laybacking: Climbing maneuver that entails pulling with the hands while pushing with the feet; also called *lieback, liebacking.*

lead: To be the first on a climb, belayed from below, and placing protection to safeguard a fall.

lieback, liebacking: See **layback, laybacking.**

line: The path of the route, usually the line of least resistance between other major features of the rock.

mantle, mantling: Climbing maneuver used to gain a single feature above your head.

mantleshelf: A rock feature, typically a ledge with scant holds directly above.

mo: See **dynamic.**

mono-doigt: A one-finger handhold, as in "mono-doigt pockets."

move: Movement; one of a series of motions necessary to gain climbing distance.

nut: A wedge or mechanical device that provides secure anchor to the rock; sometimes called a *chock.*

on-sight: To climb a route without prior knowledge or experience of the moves, without falling or otherwise weighting the rope; also called *on-sight flash.*

open grip: A handhold where the edge or pocket supports your fingers out to the second joint (or farther) and your hand lies flat against the wall.

opposition: Nuts, anchors, or climbing maneuvers that are held in place by the simultaneous stress of two forces working against each other.

"passive" nut: Nonmechanical carabiner; also see **nut** and **carabiner.**

pegs: See **pitons.**

pinch grip: A handhold where the thumb pinches in opposition to the fingers on either side of a projection.

pinkpoint: To lead (without falling) a climb that has been pre-protected with anchors rigged with carabiners.

pins: See **pitons.**

pitch: The section of rope between belays.

pitons: Metal spikes of various shapes that are hammered into the rock to provide anchors in cracks; sometimes called *pegs* or *pins*. These types of anchors were common in the 1970s but are not used much today except in aid climbing.

Marieta Akalski enjoying her vacation at El Potrero Chico, Mexico.

placement: The position of a nut or anchor.

pocket: A hole or cavity in the climbing surface used as a hold.

pocket pulling: An exhausting type of climb most often found on limestone, dolomite, and welded tuff formations.

pro: See **protection.**

problem: A short climb on a boulder accomplished without a rope.

project: A route a climber works on for a long period of time before succeeding (or not).

protection: The anchors used to safeguard the leader; sometimes called *pro.* Until the 1970s, protection devices were almost exclusively pitons. Since that time, various alloy wedges and intricate camming devices have virtually replaced pitons as generic protection devices. These wedges and cams are fitted into hollows and constrictions in cracks, and when fallen upon, actually wedge farther into the rock. In the absence of cracks, permanent bolt anchors are drilled and fitted into the rock.

prusik: Both the knot and any means by which you mechanically ascend a rope.

pulling plastic: Indoor wall climbing.

pumpy: Indicates the continuous nature of the climb.

Quad Cams: A type of spring-loaded camming devices (SLCDs), the most popular types of anchors. See **Friends.**

quickdraws: Short slings with carabiners at both ends that help provide drag-free rope management for the leader.

rack: The collection of gear a climber takes up the climb.

rappel: To descend a rope by means of mechanical brake devices.

redpoint: To lead a route, clipping protection as you go, without falling or resting on protection.

rib: A narrow buttress, not as sharp as an arête.

ring grip: A handhold where fingers are nestled close together, with the thumb wrapped over the index finger.

roof: A section of rock that extends out above your head; sometimes called a *ceiling.*

RPs: Tiny nuts used in aid climbing.

R-rated: Protection or danger rating for climbs with serious injury potential; protection may be sparse, or runout, or some placements may not hold a fall.

runner: See **sling.**

runout: The distance between two point of protection; often referring to a long stretch of climbing without protection.

sandbagging: The "shameful" practice of underestimating the actual difficulty of a given route.

second: The second person on a rope team, usually the leader's belayer.

side pull: Pulling on a vertically aligned hold to the side of the body.

signals: A set of commands used between climber and belayer.

slab: A section of rock or gentle angle, sometimes a relative reference when it's a part of a vertical wall.

SLCDs: See **spring-loaded camming devices.**

sliding nut: An anchor.

sling: A webbing loop used for a variety of purposes to anchor to the rock; used to sling gear on; sometimes called a *runner.*

smear, smearing: The climbing move of standing on the front of the foot to gain friction against the rock across the breadth of the sole in order to adhere to the rock.

"soft" rating: Rating deemed harder than the actual difficulty of a given route.

Spectra: A popular climbing rope that's stronger than nylon; also called *Spectra cord, Spectra line.*

spring-loaded camming devices (SLCDs): See **Friends.**

spring step: A climbing move where you "bounce" off your foot to propel your weight upward.

stance: A standing rest spot, often the site of a belay.

static step: A climbing move where you press your weight on one leg while simultaneously bringing your other foot up to the next hold; generally the most strenuous and least efficient way to move.

stemming: The process of counterpressuring with the feet between two widely spaced holds; sometimes called *bridging*.

"stiff" rating: Rating deemed easier than the actual difficulty of a given route; also see **sandbagging.**

stringing your nuts: Attaching a length of rope to Hexes and tapers rather than using a swaged cable.

Stoppers: Brand name of nuts made by Black Diamond.

sustained: Indicates the continuous nature of the climb.

taper: An anchor, typically in a boxy shape, that can vary from thumbnail-size micros to inch-and-a-half bombers. Variations follow four basic patterns: straight taper, curved taper, offset taper, and micro-bass or micro-steel taper.

TCUs: See **Three-Cam Units.**

TDR: See **Thermo Dynamic Rubber.**

Thermo Dynamic Rubber (TDR): A petroleum-based synthetic product used for "rubber-soled" climbing shoes.

thin: A climb or hold of relatively featureless character.

Three-Cam Units (TCUs): Spring-loaded camming devices (SLCDs) designed specifically for thin cracks. See **Friends.**

thrutch: To strain excessively; to move up, as in "layback or thrutch up a low-angle chimney."

toeing in: To edge with the shoe pointing straight on the hold, especially useful in small pockets.

toprope, toproping: A belay from an anchor point above; protects the climber from falling even a short distance.

traverse: To move sideways, without altitude gain.

tri-cam: An anchor that creates a tripod inside a crack or pocket.

undercling: Grabbing a hold with the palm up, often used as a balancing tactic until a free hand can reach above to a better hold.

wall: A long climb traditionally done over multiple days, but which may take just a few hours for ace climbers; also called a *big wall.*

work, worked, working: Refers to the expense of time and effort on numerous attempts to piece together the moves of a climb.

wrap: A handhold where the thumb is wrapped over a positive edge and the fingers are stacked on top of the thumb.

X-rated: Protection or danger rating for climbs with ground fall and death potential.

YDS: See **Yosemite Decimal System.**

Yosemite Decimal System (YDS): The usual American grading scale for identifying the technical difficulty of routes, where 5 denotes the class and the numerals following the decimal point indicate the difficulty rating, usually according to the most difficult move. Subgrades (a, b, c, and d) are used on climbs rated 5.10 and harder. When the grade is uncertain, two letters may be used (for example, a/b), which is a finer comparison of technical difficulty than the more general plus (+) and minus (–) signs.

Hallie Lee climbing *Sheila*, a 5.10a trad route in Pine Creek Canyon near Bishop, California.

appendix b:
climbing gyms

ALABAMA
Alabama Outdoors, 3054 Highway 31, Birmingham, Alabama; (800) 870-0011; www.aloutdoors.com.

Rock-It Climbing Wall, Family Fitness Center, 2100 Members Drive, Huntsville, Alabama; (256) 880-0770; www.timym.com.

ALASKA
Alaska Rock Gym, 4840 Fairbanks Street, Anchorage, Alaska; (907) 56-CRANK; www.alaskarockgym.com.

The Rock Dump, 1310 Eastaugh Way, Juneau, Alaska; (907) 586-4982; www.rockdump.com.

Cliffhanger, Wasilla Sports Complex, 105 Mack Road, Wasilla, Alaska; (907) 775-9748.

ARIZONA
Vertical Relief Climbing Center, 205 South San Francisco Street, Flagstaff, Arizona; (928) 556-9909 or (877) 265-5984; www.verticalrelief.com.

Solid Rock Gym, 23620 North 20th Drive, Suite 24, Phoenix, Arizona; (623) 587-7625.

AZ on the Rocks, 16447 North 91st Street, Suite A, Scottsdale, Arizona; (480) 502-9777; www.azontherocks.com.

Climbmax, 1330 West Auto Drive, #112, Tempe, Arizona; (480) 626-7755; www.climbmaxgym.com.

Lifetime Fitness, 1616 West Ruby Drive, Tempe, Arizona; (480) 705-8855; www.lifetimefitness.com.

Phoenix Rock Gym, 1353 East University, Tempe, Arizona; (480) 921-8322; www.phoenixrockgym.com.

Rocks and Ropes Climbing Gym, 330 South Toole Avenue, #450, Tucson, Arizona; (520) 882-5924; www.rocksandropes.com.

ARKANSAS
Little Rock Climbing Center, 12120 Colonel Glenn Road, Suite 7000, Little Rock, Arkansas; (501) 227-9500; www.littlerock climbingcenter.com.

Zion Rock Gym, 1800 Queensway, Searcy, Arkansas; (501) 368-8500; www.zionrock gym.com.

CALIFORNIA
Bladium Rock Wall, 800 West Tower Avenue, Building 40, Alameda, California; (510) 814-4999, ext. 212; www.bladium.com.

Rock City Climbing Center, 5100 East La Palma Avenue, Suite 108, Anaheim Hills, California; (714) 777-4884; www.rockcity climbing.com.

Planet Granite, 100 El Camino Real, Belmont, California; (650) 591-3030; www.planet granite.com.

Berkeley IronWorks, 800 Potter Street, Berkeley, California; (510) 981-9900; www.berkeleyironworks.com.

Rocktopia, 999 Bancroft Street, Concord, California; (925) 938-7625; www.encore gym.com/wc/htm/wc_climbing.html.

Touchstone Concord, 1220 Diamond Way, Concord, California; (925) 602-1000; http://touchstoneclimbing.com/cd.html.

Rockreation, 1300 Logan Avenue, Costa Mesa, California; (714) 555-ROCK; www.rockreation.com/cmhome.html.

Rocknasium, 720 Olive Drive, Suite Z, Davis, California; (530) 757-2902; www.rocknasium.com.

City Beach, 4020 Technology Place, Fremont, California; www.citybeach.com.

Yosemite Fitness, 5075 North Cedar Street, Fresno, California; (559) 229-ROCK.

Goleta Valley Athletic Club, 170 Los Carneros Way, Goleta, California; (805) 968-1023; www.gvac.net.

Beach City Rocks, 4926 West Rosecrans Avenue, Hawthorne, California; (310) 973-3388; www.beachcityrocks.com.

ClimbX, 18411 Gothard Street, Unit 1, Huntington Beach, California; (714) 843-9919; www.climbxhb.com.

Sunrise Rock Gym, 2455 Railroad Avenue, Livermore, California; (925) 447-8003; www.sunrisemountainsports.com.

Arcadia Rock Climbing, 305 North Santa Anita Avenue, Los Angeles, California; (626) 294-9111; www.arcadiarockclimbing.com.

Rockreation, 11866 La Grange Avenue, Los Angeles, California; (310) 207-7199; www.rockreation.com.

Stonehenge Climbing Gym, 500 Ninth Street, Modesto, California; (209) 521-3644.

Solid Rock Gym, 26784 Vista Terrace, Orange County, California; www.solidrockgym.com.

Solid Rock Gym, 13026 Stowe Drive, Poway, California; (619) 748-9011; www.solidrock gym.com.

Granite Arch Climbing Center, 11335-G Folsom Boulevard, Rancho Cordova, California; (916) 852-ROCK; www.granitearch.com.

Sacramento Pipeworks, 116 North 16th Street, Sacramento, California; www.touch stoneclimbing.com/sp.html.

Vertical Hold Sport Climbing Inc., 9580 Distribution Avenue, San Diego, California; (858) 586-7572; www.verticalhold.com.

Mission Cliffs, 2295 Harrison Street, San Francisco, California; (415) 550-0515; www.mission-cliffs.com.

Touchstone Bouldering, 200 South First Street, Suite 70, San Jose, California; (408) 920-0292; www.touchstoneclimbing.com/ sj.html.

Crux Climbing Center, 1160 Laurel Lane, San Luis Obispo, California; (805) 544-2789; www.cruxslo.com.

Slo-op Climbing, 141 Suburban Road, Suite E5, San Luis Obispo, California; www.slo-op climbing.org.

Solid Rock Gym, 992 Rancheros Drive, San Marcos, California; www.solidrockgym.com.

Class 5 Fitness, 25-B Dodie Street, San Rafael, California; (415) 485-6931; www.touchstone climbing.com/c5.html.

Sanctuary Rock Gym, 1855A East Avenue, Sand City, California; (408) 899-2595; www.rockgym.com.

Pacific Edge Climbing, 104 Bronson Street, #12, Santa Cruz, California; (831) 454-9254; www.pacificedgeclimbinggym.com.

Vertex Climbing Center, 3358A Coffey Lane, Santa Rosa, California; (707) 573-1608; www.climbvertex.com.

The Rock Gym, 2599 East Willow Street, Signal Hill, California; (562) 981-3200; www.therockgym.com.

Planet Granite, 815 Stewart Drive, Sunnyvale, California; (408) 991-9090; www.planet granite.com.

Boulderdash Indoor Rock Climbing, 880-A Hampshire Road, Suite A, Thousand Oaks, California; (805) 557-1300; www.boulder dashclimbing.com.

Hangar 18, 256 Stowell Street, Suite A, Upland, California; (909) 931-5991; www.climbhangar 18.com.

COLORADO

Boulder Rock Club and Colorado Mountain School, 2829 Mapleton Avenue, Boulder, Colorado; (303) 447-2804; www.totalclimbing.com.

The Spot, 3240 Prairie Street, Boulder, Colorado; (303) 379-8806; www.thespotgym.com.

ROCK'n & JAM'n2, 7390 South Fraser Street, Unit E, Centennial, Colorado; (303) 254-6299; www.rocknandjamn.com.

Sport Climbing Center, 4650 Northpark Drive, Colorado Springs, Colorado; (719) 260-1050; www.sportclimbcs.com.

Paradise Rock Gym, 6260 North Washington Street, Unit 5, Denver, Colorado; (303) 286-8168; www.paradiserock.com.

Thrillseekers, 1912 South Broadway, Denver, Colorado; (303) 733-8810; www.thrill seekers.com.

Animas City Rock Gym, 1111 Camino Del Rio, Durango, Colorado; (970) 259-5700; www.animascityrock.com.

Vertical Ventures, 2050 Big Thompson Avenue, Estes Park, Colorado; (970) 586-6548; www.estesparkmountainshop.com.

The Gym of the Rockies, 1800 Health Parkway, Fort Collins, Colorado; (970) 221-5000.

Inner Strength Rock Gym, 3713 South Mason, Fort Collins, Colorado; (970) 282-8118; www.innerstrengthrock.com.

Rock of Ages Climbery, Inc., 1548 Independent Avenue, Suite B, Grand Junction, Colorado; (970) 241-7622.

The Rock Climbing Center, 16240 Old Denver Highway, Monument, Colorado; (719) 481-9099; www.climbingtherock.com.

CONNECTICUT

Stone Age Rock Gym, 195 Adams Street, Manchester, Connecticut; (860) 645-0015; www.stoneagerockgym.com.

The Cliff's Climbing Gym, 91 Shelton Avenue, New Haven, Connecticut; www.climbthecliffs.com.

Go Vertical, Inc., 727 Canal Street, Stamford, Connecticut; (203) 358-8767; www.go vertical-ct.com.

Prime Climb's Mountain Fun, 340 Silversmith Park, #15, Wallingford, Connecticut; (203) 265-7880; www.primeclimb.com.

DELAWARE

The Delaware Rock Gym, 520 Carson Drive, Bear, Delaware; (302) 838-5850; www.derockgym.com.

FLORIDA

Coral Cliffs, 3400 Southwest 26th Terrace, #A4, Fort Lauderdale, Florida; (954) 321-9898; www.coralcliffs.com.

Gainesville Rock Gym, 704 South Main Street, Gainesville, Florida; (352) 335-4789; www.gainesvillerock.com.

Sun Country Rocks, 333 Southwest 140th Terrace, Gainesville, Florida; (352) 331-8773; http://suncountryrocks.com.

Aiguille Rock Climbing Center, 999 Charles Street, Longwood, Florida; (407) 332-1430; www.climborlando.com.

On the Edge Rock Climbing Gym, 200 West Drive, Melbourne, Florida; (321) 724-8775; www.ontheedgerockclimbing.com.

X-treme: The Rock Climbing Center, 13972 Southwest 139th Court, Miami, Florida; (305) 233-6623; www.x-tremerock.com.

Weatherford's Climbing Wall, 3009 East Cervantes Street, Pensacola, Florida; (850) 469-9922; www.weatherfordsoutback.com.

Tallahassee Rock Gym, 629 F Industrial Drive, Tallahassee, Florida; (850) 224-7625; www.tallyrockgym.com.

Vertical Ventures, Inc., 5402 Suite E, Pioneer Park Boulevard, Tampa, Florida; (813) 884-7625; www.verticalventures.com.

GEORGIA

Atlanta Rocks! Intown, 1019-A Collier Road, Atlanta, Georgia; (404) 351-3009; www .atlantarocks.com/intownhome.htm.

Wall Crawler Rock Club, 1522 Dekalb Avenue, #2, Atlanta, Georgia; (404) 371-8997; www.wallcrawlerrock.com.

Atlanta Rocks! Perimeter, 4411-A Bankers Circle, Doraville, Georgia; (770) 242-7625; www.atlantarocks.com/perimeterhome.htm.

Escalade Climbing Gym, 2995 Cobb Industrial Boulevard, Suite B, Kennesaw, Georgia; (770) 794-1575; www.escaladegym.com.

Reality, 125 Depot Court, Peachtree City, Georgia; (770) 487-3224; www.gorockclimb .com.

Adrenaline Climbing, 460 Brogdon Road, Suite 100, Suwanee, Georgia; (770) 271-1390; www.adrenalineclimbing.com.

IDAHO

Boise Peak Fitness, 308 South 25th Street, Boise, Idaho; (208) 363-7325; http://boise peakfitness.com.

Boise Rock Gym, 1875 Century Way, Boise, Idaho; (208) 376-3641; www.wingscenter .com.

Stonewalls Rock Gym, 751 South Capitol Avenue, Idaho Falls, Idaho; (208) 528-8610.

ILLINOIS

Rockaway Climbing Wall, 108 First Street, Batavia, Illinois; (708) 879-3636.

Upper Limits Inc., 1304 West Washington, Bloomington, Illinois; (309) 829-8255 or (800) 964-7814; www.upperlimits.com/bloomington.

LifeLines Health, Vertical Plains Climbing, Country Fair Shopping Center, 125 South Mattis Avenue, Champaign, Illinois; (217) 351-0888; www.lifelineshealth.com.

Hidden Peak, 937 West Chestnut, Chicago, Illinois; (312) 563-9400; www.lakeshore academy.com.

Lakeshore Athletic Club–Illinois Center, 211 North Stetson, Chicago, Illinois; (312) 616-9000, ext. 281; www.lsac.com/loc.php?l= ic&a=climbwall.

Oldtown Fitplex, 1235 North LaSalle, Chicago, Illinois; (312) 640-1235; www.fitness formulaclubs.com/programs/rockclimbing .php.

North Wall, 824 South Main Street, Crystal Lake, Illinois; (815) 356-6855; http://climb northwall.com.

Rox Gym, Route 26, Dixon, Illinois; (815) 288-ROX1.

Climb On, 18120 Harwood Avenue, Homewood, Illinois; (708) 798-9994; www.climbon .net.

Indoor Summits, West 290 Schoger Drive, Naperville, Illinois; (630) 585-5100, ext. 48; www.indoorsummits.com.

Sportsplex, Wolf and 159th, Orland Park, Illinois; (708) 645-PLAY; www.orland-park.il.us/recreation/html/recreat_set.html.

The Silo, 130 South John Street, Rochester, Illinois; (217) 498-9922; www.daretoclimb.com.

Vertical Endeavors, 28141 Diehl Road, Warrenville, Illinois; (630) 836-0122; www .verticalendeavors.com.

INDIANA

Hoosier Heights, 5100 South Rogers Street, Bloomington, Indiana; (812) 824-6414; www.hoosierheights.com.

Climb Time Towers, 9850 Mayflower Park Drive, Carmel, Indiana; (317) 803-2175; www.climbtimetowers.com.

Vertical eXcape, 1315 North Royal Avenue, Evansville, Indiana; (812) 479-6887; www .verticalexcape.com.

Climb Time Indy, 8750 Corporation Drive, Indianapolis, Indiana; (317) 596-3330; http://climbtimeindy.com.

IOWA

Lied Recreation Center, Iowa State University, Ames, Iowa; (515) 294-2929; www.recservices.iastate.edu/lied.

Wall-Nut Creek, 27385 530th Avenue, Kelly, Iowa; (515) 210-9940; www.iowaclimbing .com.

Long Lines Family Recreation Center, 401 Gordon Drive, Sioux City, Iowa; (712) 224-5125; www.sioux-city.org.

KANSAS

KU Rock, 208 Robinson Center, Lawrence, Kansas; (913) 841-8277.

Emerald City Gymnastics, Monster Mountain, 9063 Bond Street, Overland Park, Kansas; (913) 438-4444; www.emeraldcitygym .com/monster_mountain.htm.

Genesis Health Club, 1551 North Rock Road, Wichita, Kansas; (316) 634-0094; www.genesishealthclub.com.

Kansas Cliff Club, 4456 South Clifton, Wichita, Kansas; (316) 522-2232; www.kansascliff club.com.

North YMCA, 3330 North Woodlawn, Wichita, Kansas; www.ymcawichita.org.

KENTUCKY

Rocksport Inc., 10901 Plantside Drive, Louisville, Kentucky; (502) 266-5833; www.climb rocksport.com.

LOUISIANA

Rok Haus, 109 Grand Avenue, Lafayette, Louisiana; (337) 981-8116; www.rokhaus.com.

Slidell Rocks, 39543 Highway 190E, Slidell, Louisiana; (985) 646-1411; www.slidellrocks .com.

MAINE

Big Adventure Center, 12 North Road, Bethel, Maine; (207) 824-0929; www.big adventure.com.

Antigravity Climbing Wall, 5092 Sugarloaf Access Road, Carrabassett Valley, Maine; (207) 237-5566; www.sugarloaf.com/agc .html.

Maine Rock Gym, 127 Marginal Way, Portland, Maine; (207) 780-6370; www.merockgym .com.

North American Outdoor Adventure, Route 201, West Forks, Maine; (800) RAPIDS-9; http://northamericanoutdoor adventure.com.

MARYLAND

Earth Treks, 7125-C Columbia Gateway Drive, Columbia, Maryland; (410) 872-0060 or (800) CLIMB-UP; www.earthtreksclimbing .com.

Earth Treks, 725 Rockville Pike, Rockville, Maryland; (240) 283-9942; www.earth treksclimbing.com.

Earth Treks, 1930 Greenspring Drive, Timonium, Maryland; (410) 560-5665; www .earthtreksclimbing.com.

MASSACHUSETTS

Mill City Rock Gym, 1 Mill Street, Dracut, Massachusetts; (978) 957-1030; www .climbmillcity.com.

MetroRock #1, 69 Norman Street, Unit 9, Everett, Massachusetts; (617) 387-ROCK; www.metrorock.com.

Carabiner's Climbing Wall, 328 Parker Street, New Bedford, Massachusetts; (508) 984-0808; www.carabiners.com.

MetroRock #2, 40 Parker Street, Newburyport, Massachusetts; (978) 499-7625; www.metrorock.com.

Exxcel Gym, 88 Wells Avenue, Newton, Massachusetts; (617) 244-3300; www.exxcel.net.

NAC Rock Wallaby, Northhampton Athletic Club, 306 King Street, Northhampton, Massachusetts; (413) 585-8500; www.nohoac .com/rockwall.htm.

Gravity Rock Gym, 4 Marlboro Road, Stow, Massachusetts; (888) ROCKGYM; www.gravityrockgym.com.

Boston Rock Gym, 78G Olympia Avenue, Woburn, Massachusetts; (781) 935-7325; www.bostonrockgym.com.

MICHIGAN

Planet Rock Climbing Gym and Training Center, 82 Aprill Drive, Ann Arbor, Michigan; (734) 827-2680; www.planet-rock.com.

Inside Moves, 639 76th Street SW, Suite 2, Byron Center, Michigan; (616) 281-7088; www.insidemoves.com.

Vertical Ventures, 843 Lantern Hill Drive, East Lansing, Michigan; (517) 336-0520; http:// vertical-ventures.net.

Higher Ground Rock Climbing, 851 Bond Street NW, Grand Rapids, Michigan; (616) 774-3100; www.higround.com.

Climb Kalamazoo, 136 South Kalamazoo Mall, Kalamazoo, Michigan; (269) 385-9891; www.climbkalamazoo.com.

Planet Rock Climbing Gym and Training Center, 34 Rapid Street, Pontiac, Michigan; (248) 334-3904; www.planet-rock.com.

GT-ROCKS, 160 Hughes Drive, Traverse City, Michigan; (231) 933-7022; www.gt-rock.com.

MINNESOTA

Vertical Endeavors, 329 Lake Avenue S, Duluth, Minnesota; www.verticalendeavors .com.

Prairie Walls, 4420 19th Street NW, Rochester, Minnesota; (507) 292-0511; www.prairie walls.com.

Vertical Endeavors, 845 Phalen Boulevard, St. Paul, Minnesota; (651) 776-1430; www .verticalendeavors.com.

MISSOURI

IBEX Climbing Wall, 801 Northwest South Outer Road, Blue Springs, Missouri; (816) 228-9988; www.climbibex.com.

Petra Rock Gym, 916 North Cedarbrook, Suite C, Springfield, Missouri; (417) 866-3308; www.petrarockgym.com.

Upper Limits, 326 South 21st Street, St. Louis, Missouri; (314) 241-7625; www.upperlimits.com/stlouis.

MONTANA

Steep World, 208 North 13th Street, Billings, Montana; (406) 25-CLIMB; www.steepworld.com.

Spire Climbing Center, 13 Enterprise Boulevard, Bozeman, Montana; (406) 586-0706; www.spireclimbingcenter.com.

Helena Climbing Association, 1035 Mill Road, Helena, Montana; (406) 443-1697.

Missoula Rock Garden, 1311 East Broadway, Missoula, Montana; (406) 728-0714; www.missoularockgarden.com.

NEVADA

Nevada Climbing Centers, 3065 East Patrick Lane, Suite 4, Las Vegas, Nevada; (702) 898-8192; www.nevadaclimbingcenter.com.

Red Rock Climbing Center, 8201 West Charleston Boulevard, Suite 150, Las Vegas, Nevada; (702) 254-5604; www.redrockclimbingcenter.com.

Rock Sport Climbing Center, 1901 Silverado Boulevard, #10, Reno, Nevada; (775) 352-ROPE; www.rocksportnv.com.

NEW HAMPSHIRE

Climbing High, 68 Technology Drive, Bedford, New Hampshire; (603) 626-0311; www.climbinghigh-nh.com.

Dover Indoor Rock Climbing Wall, 47 Broadway Street, Dover, New Hampshire; (603) 742-7848; www.doverclimb.biz.

Dartmouth Climbing Gym, 113 Robinson Hall, Dartmouth College, Hanover, New Hampshire; (603) 646-1110; www.dartmouth.edu/~doc/climbinggym.

Vertical Dreams Climbing Wall, 250 Commercial Street, Fifth Floor, Manchester, New Hampshire; (603) 625-6919; www.verticaldreams.com.

Boulder Morty's, 25 Otterson Street, Nashua, New Hampshire; (603) 886-6789; www.bouldermortys.com.

Pemi Valley Rock Gym, 10 Washington Street, North Woodstock, New Hampshire; (603) 745-9800; www.pemivalleyrockgym.com.

Plymouth Rock Barn, Tenney Mountain Highway, Route 25, Plymouth, New Hampshire; (603) 536-2717.

NEW JERSEY

Up The Wall, Middlesex Gymnastics Academy, 33 McGuire Street, East Brunswick, New Jersey; (732) 249-6422; www.middlesexgymnastics.com/climbing.html.

Diamond Rock, 182 Route 10, East Hanover, New Jersey; (973) 560-0413; www.diamondrock.net.

New Jersey Rock Gym, 373D Route 46W, Fairfield, New Jersey, (973) 439-9860; www.njrockgym.com.

Rockville Climbing Center, 200 Whitehead Road, Hamilton, New Jersey; (609) 631-7625; www.rockvilleclimbing.com.

Vertical Reality, 67 Old Kings Highway, Maple Shade, New Jersey; (856) 237-1370; http://vrrockgym.tripod.com.

Rutgers University Rock Gym, College Avenue Gymnasium, 130 College Avenue, New Brunswick, New Jersey; (732) 932-5811; http://recreation.rutgers.edu/outdoors/rockwall.html.

Garden State Rocks, 705 Ginesi Drive, Morganville, New Jersey; (732) 972-3003; www.gardenstaterocks.com.

Randolph Climbing Center, 3 Middlebury Boulevard, Randolph, New Jersey; (973) 598-8555; www.randolphclimbingcenter.com.

The Gravity Vault, 107 Pleasant Avenue, Route 17N, Upper Saddle River, New Jersey; (201) 934-7625; www.gravityvault.com.

NEW MEXICO

Stone Age Climbing Wall, 4201 Yale Avenue NE, Suite 1, Albuquerque, New Mexico; (505) 341-2016; www.climbstoneage.com.

San Juan College Indoor Rock Climbing Wall, 4601 College Boulevard, Farmington, New Mexico; www.sjc.cc.nm.us/pages/1041.asp.

Lisa Hensel jamming up a
corner in Indian Creek, Utah.

Santa Fe Climbing Center, 825 Early Street, Suite A, Santa Fe, New Mexico; (505) 986-8944; www.climbsantafe.com.

NEW YORK
A.I.R.–Albany's Indoor Rockgym, 4C Vatrano Road, Albany, New York; (518) 459-7625; www.airrockgym.com.

Powerplay Recreational Center, 432 Third Avenue, Brooklyn, New York; (718) 369-9880.

The Inner Wall, Inc., 234 Main Street, Eckerd Plaza, New Paltz, New York; (845) 255-ROCK; www.theinnerwall.com.

The Rock Club, 130 Rhodes Street, New Rochelle, New York; (914) 633-7625; www.climbrockclub.com.

City Climbers Club (59th Street Gym), 533 West 59th Street, New York, New York; (212) 974-2250 or (212) 408-0277; www.cityclimbersclub.com.

Manhattan Plaza Health Club Climbing Wall, 482 West 43rd Street, New York, New York; (212) 563-7001; www.mphc.com/facilities/fac-climbing.html.

The Sports Center Climbing Wall, Chelsea Piers, Pier 60, New York, New York; (212) 336-6000; www.chelseapiers.com/fhrock.htm (Field House wall); www.chelseapiers.com/sc/climbing.htm (Sports Center wall).

Niagara Climbing Center, 1333 Strad Avenue, North Tonawanda, New York; (716) 695-1248, ext. 206; www.niagaraclimbingcenter.com.

Island Rock Gym, 60 Skyline Boulevard, Plainview, New York; (516) 822-ROCK; www.islandrock.net.

Climbing Cave, 28 Glen Drive, Queensbury, New York; (518) 798-4023.

RockSport, 138 Quaker Road, Queensbury, New York; (518) 793-4626; www.rocksportny.com.

Rock Ventures, 1044 University Avenue, Rochester, New York; (585) 442-5462; http://rockventures.net.

Electric City Rock Gym, 433 State Street, Schenectady, New York; (518) 388-2704.

The Cliffs at Valhalla, 1 Commerce Park, Valhalla, New York; (877) 914-ROCK; http://thecliffsclimbing.com.

NORTH CAROLINA
ClimbMax Inc., 43 Wall Street, Asheville, North Carolina; (828) 252-9996; www.climbmaxnc.com.

Brevard Rock Gym, 224 South Broad Street, Brevard, North Carolina; (828) 884-ROCK; www.brevardrockgym.com.

Inner Peaks Climbing Center, 9535 Monroe Road, Suite 170, Charlotte, North Carolina; (704) 844-6677; www.innerpeaks.com.

Vertical Edge Climbing Center, 2422D U.S. Highway 70, East Durham, North Carolina; (919) 596-6910; www.verticaledgeclimbing.com.

The Climbing Place, 436 West Russell Street, Fayetteville, North Carolina; (910) 486-9638; www.climbingplace.com.

RedPoint Indoor Climbing, 5213 Raeford Road, Suite 103, Fayetteville, North Carolina; (910) 868-ROCK; www.climbredpoint.com.

The Ultimate Climbing Wall, 6904 Downwind Road, Greensboro, North Carolina; (336) 665-0062; www.theultimateclimbinggym.com.

The Cornerstone, 1545 Highway 70 SW, Hickory, North Carolina; (704) 324-4653.

Sandhills Vertical Gym, P.O. Box 3780, Pinehurst, North Carolina; (910) 295-0724.

Raleigh Rock Yard, 4200 Atlantic Avenue, Raleigh, North Carolina; (919) 954-9666; http://raleighrockyard.com.

Climb On! 301 North Green Meadows Drive, Wilmington, North Carolina; (910) 794-8722; www.climbon.biz.

NORTH DAKOTA
Northern Heights Rock Climbing Gym, 1726 South Washington Avenue, Suite 42A, Grand Forks, North Dakota; (701) 795-5085.

OHIO
Climb Time, 10898 Kenwood Road, Cincinnati, Ohio; (513) 891-4850; www.ctoba.com.

Rockquest Climbing Center, 3475 East Kemper Road, Cincinnati, Ohio; (513) 733-0123; www.rockquest.com.

Vertical Adventure Rock Gym, 6295 Busch Boulevard, Columbus, Ohio; (614) 888-8393; www.verticaladventuresohio.com.

Urban Krag Indoor Rock Climbing Center, 125 Clay Street, Dayton, Ohio; (937) 224-KRAG; www.urbankrag.com.

Cleveland Rock, 21200 St. Clair, Building B3, Euclid, Ohio; (216) 692-3300; www.cleveland rockgym.com.

Vertical Reality, Gilboa Stone Quarry, off Route 224, Gilboa, Ohio; http://vertical reality.cc.

Outdoor Pursuit Center, Miami University, 700 South Oak Street, Oxford, Ohio; (513) 529-1430; www.units.muohio.edu/rsp/ RSCWeb/opc/climbingcenter.htm.

Kendall Cliffs, 60 Kendall Park Road, Peninsula, Ohio; (330) 655-5489; www.kendallcliffs.com.

Westerville Community Center, 350 North Cleveland Avenue, Westerville, Ohio; (614) 901-6500; www.westerville.org/ Default.aspx?tabid=111.

OKLAHOMA

OKC Rocks, 200 Southeast Fourth Street, Oklahoma City, Oklahoma; (405) 319-1400; www.okcrocks.com.

New Heights Rock Climbing Gym, 1140 South 107th E Avenue, Tulsa, Oklahoma; (918) 439-4400; www.newheightsgym.com.

OREGON

SOU Rock Gym, 1250 Siskiyou Boulevard, PMB 64, Ashland, Oregon; (541) 840-7245; www.aycp.org.

Stoneworks, 6775 SW 111th Avenue, Beaverton, Oregon; (503) 644-3517; www.belay .com.

Inclimb Rock Gym, 550 Southwest Industrial Way, Studio 39, Bend, Oregon; (541) 388-6764; www.inclimb.com.

Kick and Climb, 6026 Crater Lake Avenue, Central Point, Oregon; (541) 830-0824; www.kickandclimb.com.

The Crux Rock Gym, 401 West Third Avenue, Eugene, Oregon; (541) 484-9535; www.cruxrock.com.

The Ledge, 369 South Sixth Street, Klamath Falls, Oregon; (541) 882-5586.

Pull Down Climbing, 360 South H Street, Lakeview, Oregon; (541) 947-7855.

Rogue Rock Gym, 3001 Samike Drive, Suite 104, Medford, Oregon; (541) 245-2665; www.roguerockgym.com.

The Circuit Bouldering Gym, 6050 Southwest Macadam Avenue, Portland, Oregon; (503) 246-5111; www.thecircuitgym.com.

Portland Rock Gym, 21 Northeast 12th Avenue, Portland, Oregon; (503) 232-8310; www.portlandrockgym.com.

Club Sport, 18120 Southwest Lower Boones Ferry Road, Tigard, Oregon; (503) 968-4500; www.clubsports.com/oregon.

PENNSYLVANIA

Vertical Extreme, 462 Acorn Lane, Downingtown, Pennsylvania; (610) 873-9620; http:// verticalextreme.com.

The Adventure Center, 3853 Old Easton Road, Doylestown, Pennsylvania; (215) 230-9085; www.doylestownrockgym.com.

Jumonville Ben Cromer Adventure Center, 887 Jumonville Road, Hopwood, Pennsylvania; (724) 439-4912; http://jumonville .gospelcom.net/f/adv/adcenter/f.newadctr .html.

The Big Gray Rock, Lock Haven YMCA, 145 East Water Street, Lock Haven Pennsylvania; (570) 748-6727; www.lockhavenymca.com.

Climbnasium, 339 Locust North Point Road, Mechanicsburg, Pennsylvania; (717) 795-9580; www.climbnasium.net.

Milton Rock Gym, 45 South Front Street, Milton, PA; (570) 742-8290; www.miltonrock gym.com.

Philadelphia Rock Gym, 422 Business Center, Oaks, Pennsylvania; (610) 666-ROPE; www.philarockgym.com.

Go Vertical, 950 North Penn Street, Philadelphia, Pennsylvania; (215) 928-1800; www .govertical.com.

The Climbing Wall Inc., 7501 Penn Avenue, Pittsburgh, Pennsylvania; (412) 247-7334; www.theclimbingwall.com.

Reading Rocks, 1115 Bern Road, Reading, Pennsylvania; (610) 374-6007; www.reading rocks.com.

PRG Climbing Center, 255 South Mount Airy Road, Valley Township, Pennsylvania; (877) 822-ROPE; www.philarockgym.com.

Climb North, 2468 Wildwood Road, Wildwood, Pennsylvania; (412) 487-2145; www.jewarts.com/climbnorth.

Wilkes Barre Rock Climbing Gym Incorporated, 102–104 South Main Avenue, Wilkes Barre, Pennsylvania; (570) 824-7633; www.wbcg.net.

North Summit Climbing Wall, 481 Bushkill Plaza Lane, Wind Gap, Pennsylvania; (610) 863-4444; www.northsummitclimbing.com.

Reading Rocks, 1115 Bern Road, Wyomissing, Pennsylvania; (610) 374-6007; www.reading rocks.com.

RHODE ISLAND
Ocean State Rock Climbing, 3 New England Way, Lincoln, Rhode Island; (401) 333-1531; www.oceanstaterockclimbing.com.

Rhode Island Rock Climbing Gym, 100 Higginson Avenue, Lincoln, Rhode Island; (401) 727-1704; http://rhodeislandrockgym .com.

SOUTH CAROLINA
Trailhead Climbing & Outdoor Center, 505 Camson Road, Anderson, South Carolina; (864) 225-1010; www.trailheadclimbing.com.

Stronghold Athletic Club, 925 1/2 Huger Street, Columbia, South Carolina; (803) 256-9001; www.strongholdathletic.com.

Rocks and Ropes, 912 South Main Street, Greenville, South Carolina; (864) 271-9557; www.rocksandropes.net.

SOUTH DAKOTA
Dakota Rock Gym, 1830 Lombardy Drive, Rapid City, South Dakota; (605) 342-6542.

TENNESSEE
TBA Gym, 3804 St. Elmo Avenue, Suite 102, Chattanooga, Tennessee; (423) 822-6800; www.tbagym.com.

Cool Springs Climbing Center, 121 Seaboard Lane, Suite 10, Franklin, Tennessee; (615) 661-9444; www.coolspringsclimbing center.com.

The Climbing Center, 9510 Continental Drive, Knoxville, Tennessee; (865) 691-2980.

Climb Nashville, 3630 Redmon Street, Unit 1, Nashville, Tennessee; (615) 463-7625; www .climbnashville.com.

TEXAS
Dyno-Rock, 608 East Front Street, Arlington, Texas; (817) 461-3966; www.dynorock.com.

Austin Rock Gym, Inc., 4401 Freidrich Lane, Suite 300, Austin, Texas; (512) 416-9299; www.austinrockgym.com.

Exposure Indoor Rock Climbing, 2389-B Midway Road, Carrollton, Texas; (972) 732-0307; www.exposurerockclimbing.com.

Stoneworks Indoor Rock Gym, 1003 Fourth Avenue, Carrolton, Texas; (972) 323-1047; www.stoneworkssilos.com.

SMU Climbing Center, 6000 Airline Drive, SMU Rec Center, Dallas, Texas; (214) 768-9917; http://smu.edu/recsports/dedman/ expansion.html.

Canyons of Frisco, 7164 Technology Drive, Suite 202, Frisco, Texas; (214) 387-0906; www.canyonsclimbing.com.

Summit Climbing Gym, 1040 Mustang Drive, Grapevine, Texas; (817) 421-3888; www.summitrockgym.com.

Boulders Sport Climbing Center, 325 Indian Trail, Harker Heights, Texas; (254) 690-9790; www.climbboulders.com.

Outdoor Adventure, University of Houston, 4500 University Drive, Houston, Texas; (713) 743-9512; www.uh.edu/recreation/outdoor/ index.html.

Stone Moves Indoor Rock Climbing, 6970 FM 1960 W, Suite C, Houston, Texas; (281) 397-0830; www.stonemoves.com.

Texas Rock Gym–Memorial, 1526 Campbell Road, Houston, Texas; (713) 973-ROCK; http://texasrockgym.com.

Texas Tech Climbing Center, Texas Tech University, Lubbock, Texas; (806) 742-3351; www.depts.ttu.edu/recsports/outdoor/climb .php.

Elevator Rock, 400 Bridge Street, #4, Wichita Falls, Texas; (940) 767-0620; www.elevator rock.com.

UTAH

Rock Haus Indoor Climbing, 1780 North 200 East, North Logan, Utah; (435) 713-0068; www.rockhausgym.com.

The Quarry, 2494 North University Parkway, Provo, Utah; (801) 418-0266; www.the quarry.net.

The Front Climbing Club, 1450 South 400 W, Salt Lake City, Utah; (801) 466-ROCK; www.frontslc.com.

Momentum Indoor Climbing, 10600 South 220 W, Salt Lake City, Utah; (800) 896 8121; www.momentumclimbing.com.

Rockreation, 2074 East 3900, Salt Lake City, Utah; (801) 278-7473; www.rockreation.com.

VERMONT

Petra Cliffs Climbing Center, 105 Briggs Street, Burlington, Vermont ; (866) 65-PETRA; www.petracliffs.com.

The Wall–Climbing and Cafe, Route 4, Quechee, Vermont; (802) 457-2221; www .vermontrocks.com.

Green Mountain Rock Climbing Center, 223 Woodstock Avenue, Rutland, Vermont; (802) 773-3343; www.vermontclimbing.com.

Valley Rock Gym, Sugarbush Health & Racquet Club, 1840 Sugarbush Access Road, Warren, Vermont; (802) 583-6700; www .sugarbush.com.

VIRGINIA

Sportrock Climbing Centers, 5308 Eisen-hower Avenue, Alexandria, Virginia; (703) 212-7625; www.sportrock.com.

ACAC ROCKS, 629/2 Berkmar Circle, Charlottesville, Virginia; (434) 817-3800.

Peak Experiences, 11421 Polo Circle, Midlothian, Virginia; (804) 897-6800; www .peakexperiences.com.

Sportrock Climbing Centers, 45935 Maries Road, Sterling, Virginia; (571) 434-ROCK; www.sportrock.com.

Clington Climbing Inc., Tazewell Industrial Park, Tazewell, Virginia; (540) 988-7001.

Virginia Beach Rock Gym, 5049 Southern Boulevard, Virginia Beach, Virginia; (757) 499-8347; www.vbrg.com.

WASHINGTON

Vertical World–Bremerton, 5934 Highway 303 NE, Bremerton, Washington; (360) 373-6676; www.verticalworld.com.

Vertical World–Everett, 2820 Rucker Ave-nue, Everett, Washington; (425) 258-3431; www.cascadecrags.com.

Warehouse Rock Gym, 315 Jefferson Street NE, Olympia, Washington; (360) 596-WALL; www.warehouserockgym.com.

Vertical World–Redmond, 15036-B North-east 95 Street, Redmond, Washington; (425) 881-8826; www.verticalworld.com.

Stone Gardens, Inc., 2839 Northwest Market Street, Seattle, Washington; (206) 781-9828; www.stonegardens.com.

Vertical World–Seattle, 2123 West Elmore Street, Seattle, Washington; (206) 283-4497; www.verticalworld.com.

Wild Walls, Inc., 202 West Second Avenue, Spokane, Washington; (509) 455-9596; www .wildwalls.com.

Edgeworks Climbing Wall, 6102 North Ninth Street, Suite 200, Tacoma, Washington; (253) 564-4899; www.edgeworks-climbing .com.

WISCONSIN

Boulders Climbing Wall, 3964 Commercial Avenue, Madison, Wisconsin; (608) 244-8100; www.bouldersgym.com.

Turner's Climbing Alliance, 1034 North Fourth Street, Milwaukee, Wisconsin; (414) 273-1826; www.milwaukeeturners.org/turners-climbing.

Adventure Rock Indoor Rock Climbing Wall, 21250 West Capitol Drive, Pewaukee, Wisconsin; (262) 790-6800; www.adventurerock.com.

Wall Crawlers, 138 West Main Street, Whitewater, Wisconsin; (262) 473-5450; www.wallcrawlers.us.

WYOMING

The Peak, 408 North Beverly Street, Casper, Wyoming; (307) 472-4084.

Teton Rock Gym, 1116 Maple Way, Jackson, Wyoming; (307) 733-0707.

Elemental Training Center, 205 Lincoln Street, Lander, Wyoming; (307) 332-0480; www.elementaltraining.com.

Gravity Club Climbing Wall, 737 Cascade Street, Lander, Wyoming; (307) 332-6339.

Backyard Bouldering Gym, 825A Renshaw Street, Laramie, Wyoming; (307) 742-9131; www.backyardbouldering.com.

The Rock, Rock Springs Civic Center, 410 N Street, Rock Springs, Wyoming; (307) 352-1420; www.rswy.net/departments/climbingwall.htm.

appendix c:
climbing instruction

ALASKA

Mountain Trip, Anchorage, Alaska; www
.mountaintrip.com. Alaskan mountain climbs,
instruction, and private guiding.

MICA Guides, Chickaloon, Alaska; www
.micaguides.com. Ice climbing, mountaineering, and trekking on and around Matanuska
Glacier.

Alaska Mountain Guides, Haines, Alaska;
http://alaskamountainguides.com. Mountaineering, rock climbing, and ice climbing guiding and instruction. Operates in Glacier Bay
and Saint Elias National Parks.

Kennicott-McCarthy Wilderness Guides,
Kennicott, Alaska; http://kennicottguides.com.
Ice-climbing and mountaineering guiding and
seminars. Operates in the Wrangell Saint
Elias National Park.

**Rainier Mountaineering, Inc., Guide Ser-
vices,** Mount Rainier National Park, Alaska;
www.rmiguides.com. Leading guide service
in Mount Rainier National Park and also
offers guide service on Mount McKinley.

Alaska Mountaineering School, Talkeetna,
Alaska; www.climbalaska.org. Mountaineering
and ice-climbing guiding and instruction.

ARIZONA

Arizona Climbing Adventure School,
Carefree, Arizona; www.climbingschool.com.
Rock climbing instruction and guiding.

Climb Arizona, Tucson, Arizona; www.climb
arizona.com. Guided climbing and instruction.

COLORADO

Bob Culp Climbing School, Boulder,
Colorado; http://bobculp.com. Rock and ice
climbing instruction and guiding.

Colorado Mountain School, Estes Park,
Colorado; www.totalclimbing.com. Rock
climbing, ice climbing, and mountaineering
instruction and guiding. Operates in Utah,
Colorado, and Arizona.

CraigLuebben.com, Golden, Colorado;
http://craigluebben.com. Information on
guiding and instruction for all levels of rock
and ice climbing.

Colorado Mountain Guides, Nederland,
Colorado; www.cmtnguides.com. Rock
climbing instruction and guiding.

San Juan Mountain Guides, Ouray, Colorado; www.ourayclimbing.com. Mountaineering, ice climbing, and rock climbing
instruction.

Front Range Climbing Company, Parker,
Colorado; www.frontrangeclimbing.com.
Guided rock and ice climbing trips and
instruction in Colorado, Wyoming, and Utah.

GEORGIA

Granite Arches Climbing Services, Athens,
Georgia; www.granitearches.com. Rock
climbing instruction. Operates in the south-
eastern United States.

Tree Climbing USA, Fayetteville, Georgia;
www.treeclimbingusa.com. Provides history
of tree climbing and offers courses, parties,
and expeditions.

NEW YORK

**Adirondack Rock and River Guide Ser-
vice,** Keene, New York; www.rockandriver
.com. Rock and ice climbing guiding and river
sports.

Alpine Adventures, Keene, New York; www
.alpineadven.com. Instruction and guiding
for rock climbing, ice climbing, mountaineering, and backcountry skiing. Operates in the
Adirondacks.

HighXposure Adventures Inc, Ulster Park, New York; http://high-xposure.com. Rock climbing instruction.

MAINE

Acadia Mountain Guides Climbing School, Bar Harbor, Maine; www.acadiamountain guides.com. Instruction in all levels of rock and ice climbing and mountaineering as well as private guiding and international expeditions. Operates in Acadia National Park, Maine, and at peaks throughout the Americas.

Rock Climbing Camp, Bar Harbor, Maine; http://climbacadia.org/camp. Offers programs for kids and teens covering technical skills and climbing movement. Based in Acadia National Park and the White Mountains of New Hampshire.

MARYLAND

Adventure Schools, Cabin John, Maryland; www.adventureschool.com. Rock climbing instruction throughout the mid-Atlantic region.

Nirvana Climbing Guides, Point of Rocks, Maryland; www.nirvanaclimbing.com. Guided climbing and instructional courses.

MASSACHUSETTS

Top Rope, Rockland, Massachusetts; http://top-roping.com. Nonprofit organization specializing in rock climbing instruction for individuals and groups.

MONTANA

Reach Your Peak, Bozeman, Montana; http://climbmontana.com. Rock climbing, ice climbing, and mountaineering guiding and instruction.

NORTH CAROLINA

Rock Dimensions, Boone, North Carolina; www.climbnc.com. North Carolina rock climbing instruction and guiding.

Fox Mountain Guides, Hendersonville, North Carolina; www.foxmountainguides.com. Offers rock climbing trips, guide service, and instruction.

OKLAHOMA

Guide for a Day, Moore, Oklahoma; www.guideforaday.com. Guided rock climbing in Oklahoma and Arkansas.

The Climbing School, Tulsa, Oklahoma; www.theclimbingschool.com. Offers rock climbing courses in Oklahoma and Arizona plus mountaineering expeditions to the Pacific Northwest.

OREGON

Timberline Mountain Guides, Bend, Oregon; http://timberlinemtguides.com. Instructional courses and guided climbs on snow, rock, and ice.

Traditional Mountaineering, Bend, Oregon; www.traditionalmountaineering.org. Information and instruction about mountain-climbing safety skills and gear, off-trail hiking, and lightweight backpacking.

SOUTH DAKOTA

Sylvan Rocks, Hill City, South Dakota; www.sylvanrocks.com. Rock climbing instruction and guiding in the Needles and Mount Rushmore areas of South Dakota and at Devils Tower in Wyoming.

TENNESSEE

Desiderata Institute, La Vergne, Tennessee; www.warriorsway.com. Provides psychological training for rock climbers.

TEXAS

Aspire Adventures, Austin, Texas; www.climbtexas.com. Rock climbing guiding and instruction. Operates in Texas and Potrero Chico, Mexico.

Mountain Madness Climbing School, Austin, Texas; www.mtmadness.com. Rock climbing instruction and private guiding in Texas.

Rock-About, Inc., Austin, Texas; www.rock-about.com. Rock climbing instruction in Texas, Colorado, and Mexico.

UTAH

Moab Cliffs and Canyons, Moab, Utah; www.cliffsandcanyons.com. Guided climbing and canyoneering.

Moab Desert Adventures, Moab, Utah; www.moabdesertadventures.com. Rock climbing instruction and guiding.

Exum Utah Mountain Adventures, Salt Lake City, Utah; www.exum.ofutah.com. Rock and ice climbing guiding and instruction.

Frankenfield, Jim, Salt Lake City, Utah; www.mountain-guiding.com. Alpine climbing guide.

Zion Rock Guides, Springdale, Utah; www.zionrockguides.com. Offers canyoneering, rock climbing, multi-sport trips, instructional courses, guided trips, wilderness medicine classes, and search and rescue courses. Operates in Zion National Park.

Paragon Climbing Instruction, St. George, Utah; www.paragonclimbing.com. Climbing instruction and guiding.

WASHINGTON

International Mountain Guides, Ashford, Washington; www.mountainguides.com. Group and private climbing and instruction. Operates internationally.

Mount Rainier Alpine Guides, Ashford, Washington; www.mountainguides.com. Offers mountaineering training programs and guided ascents of Mount Rainier.

Cascade Alpine Guides, Sammamish, Washington; www.cascadealpineguides.com. Offers guided summit climbs on Mount Rainier and other peaks in the Cascades as well as guided treks in the Havasupai Grand Canyon.

WEST VIRGINIA

Seneca Rocks Climbing School, Seneca Rocks, West Virginia; www.seneca-rocks.com. Rock climbing instruction and private guiding.

WISCONSIN

Humphrey Essential Skills Outdoor School, Viroqua, Wisconsin; www.essentialskills.org. Offers rock climbing programs.

WYOMING

Devils Tower Above All, Devils Tower, Wyoming; www.devilstowerclimbing.com. Guiding and rock climbing instruction in the Devils Tower area.

Tower Guides, Devils Tower, Wyoming; www.towerguides.com. Rock and ice climbing instruction and guiding in Wyoming, Colorado, South Dakota, and Utah.

Jackson Hole Mountain Guides, Jackson, Wyoming; www.jhmg.com. Rock climbing instruction and guiding. Operates in the Grand Tetons, the Beartooths, and the Wind Rivers.

appendix d:
female-oriented rock climbing events

Chicks on Cracks: Moab Desert Adventures, www.moabdesertadventures.com. Improve your traditional climbing skills with experienced female climbing instructors. A unique opportunity for climbers is offered: learning to crack climb in the world's foremost crack-climbing destination, Indian Creek, Utah.

Exum Women's Climbing/Mountaineering/Ski Camps, www.womenspecific.com/camps/show/10. Offers Desert West and Rockies guided ice climbing, mountaineering, rock climbing, and telemark skiing, all of which can be arranged to be women specific. Total novices are welcome. They also guide any peak or route in Grand Teton National Park, the Wind Rivers, Devils Tower, City of Rocks (Idaho), and the Needles (South Dakota).

Girls Adventure Out, www.womenspecific.com/camps/show/12. Desert West and Pacific Northwest backpacking, rock climbing, surfing, and wilderness survival/backcountry expeditions are offered.

"Goddesses On The Rocks" Women's Climbing Weekends, www.sterlingrope.com. Climbing clinics instructed by female athletes. Sponsored by Sterling Rope.

Lynn Hill Climbing Camps, www.lynnhillclimbs.com/. Work on skills that will help prepare you for a variety of climbing styles—crack climbing, technical face climbing, sport climbing, or bouldering—in camps designed to give you a comprehensive experience that will help you become more conscious and efficient in your climbing.

Mind Over Mountains: Thought-Provoking Adventures, www.womenspecific.com/dailyfeed/show/45. Nestled in the heart of the San Juan Mountains of Colorado, thought-provoking adventures combine hiking, yoga, rock climbing, life coaching, stimulating workshops, and spa services for women of all ages. No prior experience is necessary.

The Women's Wilderness Institute, www.womenspecific.com/camps/show/22. High-quality outdoor adventures for women and teenage girls in the Rocky Mountains and southwestern deserts and rivers, including rock climbing, mountain biking, backpacking, backcountry yoga retreats, canoeing, fly fishing, and wilderness writing workshop.

about the author

As the first woman to on-sight 5.13d (*Omaha Beach,* Red River Gorge, Kentucky) and flash 5.14a (*Hydrophobia,* Mont Sant, Spain), Katie Brown has been an influential and ground-breaking climber. She began climbing at age thirteen and quickly dominated competition at the national and international level. Now in her twenties, she is a freelance writer and continues to travel the world as a professional climber.

Katie Brown liebacking a sandstone crack near Moab, Utah.

Point.
Click.
Send.

Climbing.com